The New Local Authorities

management and structure

*Report of a study group appointed jointly by the Secretary of State for the Environment and local authority associations * to examine management principles and structures in local government at both elected member and officer levels.*

Presented to the Secretary of State and the Associations August 1972

*   *The Association of Municipal Corporations*
The County Councils' Association
The Rural District Councils' Association
The Urban District Councils' Association

LONDON HER MAJESTY'S STATIONERY OFFICE 1972

Published for the Department of the Environment

SBN   11 750530 7

The Study Group on Local Authority Management Structures

Steering Committee

Chairman: Sir Frank Marshall (City of Leeds)

Association of Municipal
Corporations: A Lloyd-Allen (Poole)
A G Taylor
(London Borough of Sutton)
J C Swaffield (Secretary)

County Councils' Association: Sir Geoffrey Shakerley (Glos)
J M Whittaker (North Riding)
C C Barker (Herts)
A C Hetherington (Secretary)

Rural District Councils'
Association: C Sellick (Bridgwater)
J S Cripps (Witney)
S Rhodes (Secretary)

Urban District Councils'
Association: J McKnight (Welwyn Garden City)
W H Coleman (Gelligaer)
W R Warrington (Secretary)

Department of the Environment: J E Hannigan

Other Members: Sir Cyril Kleinwort, (Chairman,
Kleinwort, Benson Lonsdale, Ltd)

M Horsman (Chairman, Ralli
International Ltd)

Working Group

Chairman: M A Bains   *Clerk of the Kent County Council*

Members: J E Bolton   *Clerk of the Barrow-on-Soar Rural District Council*

                   H D Jeffries   *Clerk of the Beeston and Stapleford Urban District Council*

                   J V Miller   *County Treasurer, Gloucestershire County Council*

               * R G Morgan   *Town Clerk (Designate), Brighton County Borough Council*

                  G C Moore   *Town Clerk, Bradford County Borough Council*

              † A G Woods   *Company Secretary, Imperial Chemical Industries Ltd*

                            * *Formerly Borough Treasurer*

                            † *Now retired*

Secretary to the
Study Group: M J Wanstall

To: **The Secretary of State for the Environment**
The Association of Municipal Corporations
The County Councils' Association
The Rural District Councils' Association
The Urban District Councils' Association

The Study Group on Local Authority Management Structures was set up by you in May 1971 to produce advice for the new local authorities on management structures at both member and officer level. It is my pleasure, on behalf of the Study Group, to present to you this report, prepared by the Working Group under the general direction of the Steering Committee. We hope that it will assist those whose task it will be to determine appropriate management principles and structures within the new authorities.

Frank Marshall (Chairman)

Foreword

by the Secretary of State for the Environment
The Rt. Hon. P. E. Walker, M.B.E., M.P.

I look upon this report as being one of the most important and vital aspects of local government reform. Local government tends to be only reformed once a century and we therefore have a unique opportunity to study carefully the best management practices within local government and to see that these practices are in the future carried out by all.

The report contains a wealth of practical advice. If every newly elected member and every newly appointed officer of the new authorities studies this report carefully and sees that those suggestions appropriate are applied to the work of his new authority then local government in the future is going to be far more efficient and effective than ever before.

The members of the working group have been outstandingly diligent in their efforts to make this a document of sound practical advice. I could not be more grateful to them and those that have allowed them to do this work. Likewise, the local electors will be grateful to you, the reader of this document, if you make sure that the greatest possible use is made of the suggestions and advice that are now made available.

Acknowledgments

We wish to acknowledge our debt to all the individuals and bodies who have given us their assistance in our work. We recognise and appreciate that the impending reorganisation of local government has placed considerable burdens on both members and officers of all local authorities and wish, therefore, to express particular gratitude to those upon whose time we have trespassed.

We are grateful to the authorities, organisations and individuals listed in Appendices B and C who submitted written evidence to us and to those listed in Appendix E who gave oral evidence. The latter particularly were often asked to attend before us at extremely short notice and did so willingly. We are conscious that we were not able to take oral evidence from all who had offered to expand upon their written evidence, but are nonetheless grateful for those offers.

Members of the Working Group visited a number of local authorities (listed in Appendix D) and we would like to express our thanks to all who had any part in the arrangements for those visits. They proved to be of great value in our deliberations. We are grateful for the welcome and hospitality which we received and for the knowledge and information which we gained from all who answered our many questions.

We are indebted to those who gave up their time to attend the two-day seminar which we held on the 20/21 January 1972 and to the Institute of Local Government Studies at Birmingham University who assisted us with arrangements.

The expert advisers listed in Appendix F who were appointed to assist us have provided us with forthright and valuable opinions on the various matters which we have referred to them and our thanks are due to them.

The Group thank the London Borough of Lambeth for releasing on a part time basis Mr. Philip Carrington to assist the Secretariat.

Finally we wish to express our sincere thanks to our Secretary Mr. Michael Wanstall whose constructive help and criticism we have truly valued. Notwithstanding the urgency which has accompanied the preparation of our report Mr. Wanstall and his small supporting staff have cheerfully accepted the demands we have made upon them providing everything the Group have required for their discussions and successfully keeping track of the enormous amount of paper which accumulated. The Group are similarly indebted to Mr. Edward Osmotherly for his help in the preparation of the Interim Report.

Contents

Chapter 5   The organisation at officer level

Chapter 6   Personnel Management

Chapter 7   **Other central functions**

Chapter 8   **Working arrangements between the new authorities—the community approach**

Chapter 9   The new authorities—functions and possible management structures

Appendices

Preface

We see reorganisation as an opportunity which must not be missed for local government to go forward vigorously into the 21st Century. We therefore urge new authorities to be bold and resolute when setting up their management structures.

The main principles upon which our report is founded are:

1 Role of members and officers

There must be clear understanding by members and officers of their respective roles so they can forge an effective partnership. Though there can be no simple definition each must accept that the other has a legitimate interest in all aspects of the working of the authority. A "them and us" attitude fosters distrust and dissipates effectiveness.

2 The aims of the individual member

Members have a wide diversity of aims and interests. The management structure should enable every member to find satisfaction in fulfilling his particular desires. The constituency role of members is as important as the policy making role.

3 Monitoring and reviewing performance

An area of activity almost totally ignored in local government yet one of the greatest importance. The member has a vital role. Any management structure must make provision for securing value for money.

4 Effective and efficient decision-making

To encourage effective and efficient decision-making and to project a businesslike image there must be a logical pattern of delegation. All decisions should be taken at the lowest practicable level. There must be full acceptance of the principles of delegation to officers. At the same time we urge the creation of informal groups of members to provide a point of reference for officers and enable members to participate meaningfully in the affairs of the authority.

5 The corporate approach

The ingrained departmental approach to management is no longer appropriate. We urge authorities to adopt a corporate approach to their affairs in order to ensure that their resources are most effectively deployed. They have an overall interest in the economic, cultural and physical well-being of their communities and should set up consultative machinery for frequent discussions with other local authorities and statutory organisations.

6 Policy and Resources Committee

To assist the formulation and carrying out of the overall plan for the community, there should be a Policy and Resources Committee. Such a Committee would aid the authority in setting objectives and priorities, co-ordinating and controlling the implementation of those objectives, and monitoring and reviewing performance—to which we attach so much importance.

7 Chief Executive

Each authority should appoint a Chief Executive who should be of outstanding managerial ability and personality. His role would be very different from that of the traditional Clerk. Free of all departmental responsibilities, he would clearly be the head of the paid officials; he would lead a team of Chief Officers to secure overall co-ordination and control and, in many ways, would set the whole tone and tempo of the authority.

8 Personnel

There must be a much greater awareness of the importance of personnel management in local government. Manpower is a leading resource of any authority and must be properly deployed. The appointment of the senior officer responsible for personnel management is crucial and must be made at an early date.

We give a warning—whilst 1st April 1974 may seem distant, if all the necessary preparations are to be carried out in an orderly manner they must proceed with all possible speed. The new local authorities which will make the greatest impact in the shortest possible time will be those who started their preparations first.

Chapter 1

Origins, terms of reference and purpose of the study

1.1 The Working Group was appointed on 19 May 1971 by the Secretary of State for the Environment, The Association of Municipal Corporations, The County Councils' Association, The Rural District Councils' Association and the Urban District Councils' Association to produce, under the general direction of the Steering Committee, advice on management structures for the new local authorities to be set up under the reorganisation of local government. Our terms of reference were:—

'To set out the considerations which, in the Group's opinion, should be borne in mind by local authorities in determining their structures of management at elected member and officer levels including particularly internal arrangements bearing on efficiency in the employment of manpower; to inform them of experience gained by existing authorities which have given special attention to their structures of management in recent years; and indicating which patterns, in the Group's judgment, are most likely to be suitable for the types of authority to be established by the legislation now contemplated.'

1.2 At the request of the Steering Committee we produced, on 16 September 1971, a separate report on matters within our terms of reference on which we thought our views would be helpful to the Government while they were still preparing the legislation on the reorganisation of local government. A copy of that report appears at Appendix A and we make further reference to it later in this report.

1.3 In considering how to go about our main task, we have from the outset been very conscious of the importance of the time factor. Our first meeting was held on 1 July 1971 and we were originally requested to make our report by the end of 1972. We have, however, become increasingly convinced, both from our own experience and from views expressed to us, that if our report is to be of use to local authorities during the all important formative period, then it must be available well before that date. This has inevitably meant that our whole timescale has been shortened and we hope that those whose offer to expand orally the evidence which they submitted has not been taken up will understand the situation. In submitting our report at this time we are aware that some authorities, through joint committees set up to examine the problems of reorganisation, have already come to provisional conclusions as to their structures of management; indeed some had done so before we commenced the drafting of our report. If we had delayed the submission of our report there was, in our view, a very real possibility that it would have come too late to be of use to many of those concerned with the structures of the new authorities.

1.4   We were advised that our report should be essentially a manual of practical advice and we have therefore concentrated our efforts on seeking evidence and opinion from those with practical experience of the problems of restructuring management in the local government context.

1.5   In order to provide a framework within which we could pursue our study we identified nine areas of management which seemed to us to be particularly important viz:

(i) role of elected members and officers;

(ii) functions of committees and sub-committees, including any central policy committee;

(iii) relationships between officers, including the duties of any chief executive officer;

(iv) corporate planning and its implementation;

(v) departmental groupings and structures;

(vi) use and limitations of management services;

(vii) working arrangements between authorities;

(viii) collection and dissemination of information within authorities and to outside bodies and the general public;

(ix) implementation of organisational changes.

1.6 We invited evidence under these headings from seventy five professional societies and associations, staff interests, academic institutions and Government departments. We also received unsolicited evidence from a number of sources. A list of those who submitted written evidence is at Appendix B.

1.7 In addition to this we also wrote to forty local authorities, asking for

i) a factual description of their present organisation;

ii) details of any changes which had taken place in that organisation, and the reasons for them;

iii) an assessment of the strengths and weaknesses of that organisation from the Clerk or Chief Executive, an elected member and a Chief Officer respectively.

A list of authorities who responded to our letter is at Appendix C.

1.8 Members of the Working Group visited nineteen local authorities and had valuable discussions with elected members, senior officers, staff representatives and, on one occasion, representatives of the local press. A list of authorities visited is at Appendix D. In association with the Institute of Local Government Studies at Birmingham University we held a two day seminar at which we heard the views of a number of younger officers at second or third tier level. Members of the Group also visited courses at the Institute to participate in the discussion of management issues.

1.9 Oral evidence was heard from a wide range of witnesses, some of whom had, in their written evidence, sought the opportunity to expand the views which they had expressed and others who appeared before us at our request. A list of those who gave oral evidence to the Group is at Appendix E. In all we sat for a total of sixty four days between 1 July 1971 and 14 July 1972.

Chapter 2

Local government management—
its nature and purpose

2.1   There undoubtedly exists a body of opinion which infers, from our appointment, that there is very little right with local government management and administration. We would like to make it clear from the outset that this is not a view to which we generally subscribe. As in other fields of management there are wide variations in the efficiency of local authorities, but we believe that at its best local authority management compares favourably with management in other fields.

2.2   This, however, does not mean that local government generally is entitled to be complacent about its management systems and expertise. The management structures of many local authorities remain those which emerged from the development of local government in the 19th century. Reorganisation provides a unique opportunity for local government to take a critical look at itself and to make changes which might not be possible at any other time.

2.3   Our task, as we see it, is to act as a catalyst in this process of critical self examination, and to offer advice and suggestions, based mainly on the lessons of practical experience, which may assist the new authorities in creating a system of management which will lead to the most effective service to the community. We believe that a number of traditional practices should be challenged, for example the widespread involvement of elected members in day to day administration and the consequent misuse of the committee system and the failure of officers to develop and display a corporate approach to the business of the authority. We accepted the view of our Steering Committee that we should pay particular attention to the lack of machinery to ensure value for money.

2.4   The evidence which we have received and the visits which we have made to a wide range of authorities, have supported our view that there is no one perfect system of management in local government, any more than in any other sphere of activity. The needs and priorities of individual areas differ widely; they will change from time to time and local government administration must be sufficiently flexible and adaptive to meet those changing needs.

2.5 Neither are we convinced that it is possible to apply straight business concepts to management in local government. Local government may well have lessons to learn from industry, but one must be wary of attempting wholesale transplants from one to the other. To pursue the analogy, the rejection factor will be extremely high because of the different nature of the constraints within which management must operate in the two fields.

2.6 In particular the dual nature of management in local government must be recognised, but not, we hope, allowed to undermine the efficient running of the organisation. In the democratic context in which local government must operate, there are two elements both trying to "manage", i.e. elected members and officers, too often suspicious and critical of each other's role, and although friction and competition may aid efficiency they have in some authorities been allowed to impair both morale and efficiency. We believe that it is one of our major tasks to try to clarify the relationship between members and officers in order to promote an efficient and harmonious working relationship.

2.7 It is not our intention, in this report, to go again over all the ground covered by the Maud and Mallaby Committees, though many of the criticisms made by those Committees remain appropriate. We have in mind specifically the criticism of the absence of unity in the internal organisation of a local authority:—

"The separateness of the committees contributes to the separateness of departments, and the professionalism of departmental staff feeds on this separateness" (Report of the Committee on the Management of Local Government—Vol. 1 Para. 224).

Despite the efforts of some local authorities this remains, in our view, generally true.

2.8 That same Committee also recommended that the largest councils should have no more than 75 members (para. 332) and suggested that any lack of contact between the elector and the elected member would be better remedied by reducing the demands on the time of the member in committee work than by increasing the number of members in any authority. We have received a great deal of evidence, both from elected members and officers, that many councils are already too large in membership for effective management, particularly in authorities which have followed Maud's advice and reduced the number of committees. We view with considerable concern the Government proposals which will in many cases result in councils with a membership of more than 100. This, we believe, can only exacerbate the problems and difficulties which are already being encountered.

2.9   We have referred in an earlier paragraph to the importance of the member/officer relationship. We have also given much attention to the relationship between the traditional professionalism of local government and its administration. It must be recognised that at senior levels, particularly in the larger authorities, management skills are as important as professional skills and appointments to senior positions should be made on that basis.

2.10 Before attempting to decide on the structural form for any organisation it is essential to have a clear idea of the objectives and functions of that organisation. Local government is not, in our view, limited to the narrow provision of a series of services to the local community, though we do not intend in any way to suggest that these services are not important. It has within its purview the overall economic, cultural and physical well-being of that community, and for this reason its decisions impinge with increasing frequency upon the individual lives of its citizens.

2.11 Because of this overall responsibility and because of the inter-relationship of problems in the environment within which it is set, the traditional departmental attitude within much of local government must give way to a wider-ranging corporate outlook. This corporate approach should be displayed not only within the authority itself but also in its relations with other spheres of local government and with public bodies such as the proposed Area Health Boards and Regional Water Authorities. The allocation of functions to the different local authorities and the freedom given to them to create organisations which are appropriate to local needs only serve to emphasise the need for close co-ordination at all levels for the benefit of the community.

2.12 We believe that the need for a corporate approach is beyond dispute if local government is to be efficient and effective. We recognise that there are widely differing views on how it can be achieved, but it will not be sufficient merely for this principle to be recognised. A framework must be built into the organisation of the various public services within which the idea can take root and develop.

2.13 We have commented in an earlier paragraph on the effect of the decisions of local authorities upon the lives of the individual members of the community which they serve. It is important to remember that management is not an end in itself. Changes in management structure or process must be justified in terms of the benefit to the community, for in the last analysis it is to the community that local government is accountable. In the business world management relates to the maximisation of profits; in local government management is about, and more important, for people.

Chapter 3

The role of elected members and officers

Introduction

3.1   We have already emphasised the importance for the efficiency and effectiveness of the authority of the relationship between members and officers. In this chapter we attempt to establish what that relationship should be and how it should be reflected in the structure and systems of the authority.

3.2   The Maud Committee exploded the myth of policy being a matter for the elected members and administration for officers and it is disturbing to find, five years later, that many members and officers still see this as a sufficient description of their respective roles and one behind which they can shelter as occasion requires. It is perhaps even more disturbing to see how a rigid interpretation of the role of one or the other defeats any attempt to create a sense of unity of purpose within an authority.

3.3   We believe that if local government is to have any chance of achieving a corporate approach to its affairs members and officers must both recognise that neither can regard any area of the authority's work and administration as exclusively theirs.

3.4   Officers must accept that members have a legitimate interest in the day to day administration of cases involving their constituents and that it is frequently only a lack of information which causes them to pursue such matters into the administrative machine.

3.5   Members must equally realise that the skilled professional officer is not just a servant who is paid to do as he is told. We do not dispute that the major policy decisions must be taken by the elected members, but the officers have a role to play in the stimulation and formulation of policy and in seeing that the members have available the necessary advice and evaluation to enable them to make the best decisions.

3.6   How, then, do we see the respective roles working out in practice? We deal first with the elected member.

The elected member—his aims and objectives

3.7   The Maud Report recognised (para 492)   that members do not all achieve satisfaction from the same type of role within the authority and drew attention specifically to the distinction between broad policy matters and work relating to individual persons.

3.8   We believe that members of local authorities have a wide diversity of aims and interests. In addition to those who wish to take part in broad policy decisions there are, for example:—

  i)   those interested in the welfare type of activity;

  ii)   those who see it as their role to 'manage' the local authority, often by rigid application of commercial principles;

  iii)   those who wish to serve the community, in the general sense;

  iv)   those whose main objective is to limit spending by the authority.

Other categories can no doubt be identified.

3.9   If members have these diverse aims, it seems to us to.be impossible to cast them all in the same role. We suggest that the structure of the authority should be such as to provide members with work of the appropriate type and should encourage them to identify for themselves the area in which they wish to work.

3.10 As a corollary it should be recognised that the present tendency to grade the various areas of work from 'policy' as the most important to 'constituency' as the least important inevitably leads to dissatisfaction and inefficient use of qualities which individual members bring to the work of the authority. If determination of broad policy is regarded as the most important job to which any member can aspire, then it follows that those members who do not find themselves directly involved in the central policy-making processes will be jealous of the power role which they perceive being played out by those who are. They will frequently seek to use (or abuse) the Council meeting merely to emphasise where final power lies.

3.11 If members are to accept this concept of differing areas of necessary work then the structures and systems of the authority must be geared to allow them to develop and gain satisfaction from whichever role they are most suited to play. To this end the information and communication systems in particular need to become more flexible and responsive to the needs of the individual member.

3.12 We have received a considerable volume of evidence about the role of the elected member, much of which follows the general principles outlined in the Maud Report that

    a)   ultimate direction and control of the affairs of the authority should lie with the members;

    b)   the members should take the key decisions on the objectives of the authority and on the plans to attain them;

    c)   the members should keep under review the progress and performance of the services.

3.13 We would not wish to dissent from the view that all of these are functions proper to members, but, as we have already implied we doubt whether it is possible to divide the total management process into two separate halves, one for members and the other for officers. If it is to the community that local government is accountable for the effectiveness of its operations, then it is unlikely that one can rule out the elected representatives of that community from any particular part of the management process.

3.14 Mr J B Woodham suggested to us that the two elements in local government management are in fact likely to be present at every stage of the management process. That process itself can be seen as a scale, with the setting of objectives and allocation of major resources at one end, moving through the designing of programmes and plans, to the execution of those plans at the other end.

3.15 As one moves through that management scale, the balance between the two elements changes from member control with officer advice at the 'objective' end to officer control with member advice at the 'execution' end.

3.16 This seems to us to be a helpful description of the changing relationship between officers and members at the different stages of the management process. It recognises that the elected member is involved at any stage but also makes clear that at the 'execution' end of the scale it is the responsibility of the officers to see that effect is given to the decisions taken by the members and that services are effectively and efficiently managed.

3.17 We would now like to consider the member's role in a number of specific areas of activity.

The constituency role

3.18 The first of these is his role as a representative of his constituency. We have already commented on the fact that, due to lack of information, members often find it necessary to pursue constituency matters into the administrative machine. It is basic to the democratic principle that members should have full information on matters affecting their electoral area and we recommend that authorities should ensure that a member is kept fully supplied with up-to-date information on all aspects of the Council's activities, and, more specifically, with information on matters which will affect the interests of those living in his electoral area.

3.19 The flow of information between elected member and electorate should be a two way process and the member must be sufficiently well informed to be able to explain the Council's actions and policies to his constituents and feed back reaction to appropriate points within the authority organisation.

3.20 We have received evidence from a number of authorities where it is clear that there are obstacles put in the way of the 'opposition' members with regard to the obtaining of information, and we have been told of instances where chief officers have refused to give information to opposition members. Furthermore some members currently in opposition, irrespective of party, have voiced the opinion that there is too much co-operation and too much freedom of access to information—they prefer the maxim 'If you're in power you're in, and if you're out, you're out', and would clearly adopt a more restrictive attitude if they were in power.

3.21 We believe that a free flow of information not only oils the wheels of democracy; it also goes some considerable way to eliminate mistrust and misunderstanding. We accept that party politics is likely to play an increasing part in local government, but we deplore any restriction on the supply to elected members generally of information which is reasonably available.

Policy formulation and resource allocation

3.22 The second specific area which we wish to examine is that of policy formulation and decision-making, with which we include such matters as the identification of needs, the setting of objectives, establishment of priorities and allocation of resources.

3.23 These areas are recognised as primarily the responsibility of members, though, as we have pointed out earlier, the officer has a vital role to play. We do not believe that the formulation of policy should be regarded as solely within the competence of a central policy committee. There are matters upon which it is wholly appropriate for the other committees to formulate policy relating to the services for which they are responsible. 'Policy' is not something which is wholly removed from the general body of members.

3.24 Some policy changes will inevitably be in the nature of a reaction to outside events and it is therefore necessary that the policy framework within which either a committee or the authority as a whole operates should be sufficiently flexible to cope with such changes. But we believe that, essentially, policy decisions should be based on planning and analysis of objectives and the means of attaining them. Policy once made should not be regarded as immutable, and there should be a continuous process of review and re-examination, with factual evaluation of alternatives supplied by the officers.

3.25 It is impossible to foresee the situation in which a local authority will have sufficient resources, whether of money, land or manpower, to meet all the demands placed upon it by the community and the establishment of priorities and allocation of resources is therefore of critical importance. In many authorities, however, this process is still totally irrational. Committee estimates are cut all round in order to keep within what is regarded as an acceptable level of total expenditure, with no attempt made to evaluate the relative consequences of cuts in the different services which those estimates represent.

3.26 The establishment of priorities and allocation of resources requires, in our view, an overall plan against which the recommendations of committees can be measured. The process also requires more sophisticated budgeting and forward planning, a process in which not only the Treasurer, but the Chief Executive and all chief officers must play a part.

3.27 Because of the overall limitation imposed by the availability of money to finance the policies of the authority, we believe that the policy and finance functions must be linked at member level. It has been suggested to us that policy should be determined according to idealistic criteria and that financing is a separate exercise which should not be allowed to determine policy. According to this argument, it follows that finance and policy should be separated in the structure of committees. We believe that such a separation presents substantial problems of co-ordination and that the examination of ideals against financial constraints is more effectively done by the one body.

Monitoring and review

3.28 The third area upon which we wish to comment specifically is the role of the elected member in the process of monitoring and reviewing of performance.

3.29 The evidence which we have received suggests that whilst this is generally recognised as an important part of the role of the elected member, little opportunity is given to him to review procedures and monitor progress except when the occasional 'disaster' forces something into the limelight.

13

3.30 Some of the newer management techniques and systems, particularly PPBS, require monitoring and review as a built-in part of the system from which judgments are made and policies altered and the very fact that it is built into the system ensures that the function is not neglected.

3.31 Financial stringency has, almost incidentally, led to more attention being paid to monitoring and review by restricting the resources available for growth. The result has been that committees have been forced to examine critically the necessity for and effectiveness of current activities in order to find savings with which either to promote new activities or expand particular existing ones.

3.32 In order to assist and encourage this process, greater attention must be paid to the development of methods of assessing the effectiveness of activities against which progress and performance can be measured. For too long the main criterion of success has been the amount of resources put into a particular service with but little regard for its output.

3.33 This 'watchdog' function, is, we suggest, very much one for the elected member, both through membership of the particular committee responsible for the service under review, and through his more general role as a representative of the community to whom the authority is accountable for the effective use of its resources.

The officer's role

3.34 We now turn to the role of the officer. We have already referred to the dual nature of management in local government and to the need for officers and members to accept that each has a contribution to make. It may seem unnecessary for us to reaffirm that they cannot be placed in separate watertight compartments, but we do so to emphasise that both should be working in partnership towards a common end. Mutual confidence and respect can only lead to better decision making and, therefore, to a better service to the electorate. At the individual level, objectives and motivation will differ widely, and may well change from time to time according to personal or other circumstances but this does not, we believe, invalidate the concept of a corporate approach between officers and members collectively.

The 'professionalism' of local government

3.35 Before discussing the role of the officer, there is a general point which we feel needs to be made. The local government service at officer level is based upon a tradition of professional skills, each operating within its own specialism. As new functions have been given to local government to perform, so new 'professions' have grown up, each with its own professional body to develop and improve the skills of its members, but often becoming increasingly concerned with the status of that particular profession in relation to others. We have received evidence from a very wide range of professional bodies in local government and, whilst many have made extremely valuable and constructive suggestions, sometimes bending over backwards to avoid any special pleading on behalf of their own profession, there have been others whose whole approach to the subject appears to have been conditioned by the desire to preserve their position in relation to other professions.

3.36 We believe that the 'professionalism', in its widest sense, of the local government service is one of its major strengths and that the professional bodies can take much of the credit for the high level of skills now exercised by their members, but we have been concerned at the introverted approach of some professional bodies as revealed by their evidence to us. We discuss in a later chapter the problems of 'departmentalism' within authorities and we believe that local government should also be on its guard against over-emphasis on the narrow concept of professionalism which seems to us to be still developing.

3.37 In the preceding chapter we have already made some brief comments on the role of the officer. Our terms of reference require us to pay particular regard to efficiency in the employment of manpower and this is nowhere more important than at the level of the chief officers in their relationship with members. As we have already said officers are not paid just to do as they are told. They must be allowed to advise on policy formulation and take decisions within a policy framework laid down by the members either in Council or in committee.

They are skilled men, trained specifically for the work of a local authority and should be given responsibility and authority accordingly. This, of course, brings us back to our point about mutual confidence and respect, because without the trust and confidence of the members, officers' skills will become under-utilised and the officers themselves will lack motivation and impetus. Our visits to local authorities have demonstrated clearly the benefit of vesting the officers with the authority to get on with the job which they are paid to do.

Delegation to officers

3.38 It has been suggested that extensive delegation to officers is in some way undemocratic, but we do not accept this, provided that the terms of delegation are clear and specific. For example, in many authorities the principles under which the allocation of housing is to be made are laid down by the Housing Committee and the Housing Manager then operates the system within those principles under delegated powers. There are, however, other authorities where the members make the allocation on the principle that it would be undemocratic to leave the matter to an officer. This we believe generally to be inefficient, not in the sense that the members' decisions are wrong, but because the process will inevitably be slower and because the knowledge and skill of a trained officer are not being properly used. The democratic principle is, in our view, protected by the right of members to withdraw or amend the powers given to the officer; as Mr R G E Peggie put it in a paper which he delivered to the 1971 LAMSAC National Conference*, the elected member "... should be concerned to ensure that the machine works, but he should not be required to operate it himself".

3.39 It is a basic principle of management that responsibility and authority must coincide and it follows that if officers are given the authority to take decisions they must also accept the responsibility for the consequences of those decisions. We have found that many committee agendas are liberally sprinkled with matters which seem to us to be manifestly suitable for decision at officer level, though whether this is as a result of pressure from the members or a reluctance on the part of the officers to act decisively is a matter which requires closer analysis at local level than we have been able to give. What

* LAMSAC National Conference Report 1971, pp. 240-252

is clear is that as a result there is often too little time available in committee to give the really important matters the attention which they warrant.

3.40 We do not believe that delegated authority, once given, requires a constant stream of reports back to the delegating committee. The officer's task is to get on with the job which he has been given to do and having given him the necessary powers the committee should allow him to exercise them according to his own judgment. He is, of course, accountable for the decisions which he takes, but such accountability, in our view, should be checked by review and investigation techniques, where the decision as to the subject of review rests with the reviewing body and is not decided by what is, or is not, included in routine written reports.

3.41 An officer working under delegated powers needs, nevertheless, to keep in close touch with the committee responsible for the function which he is performing. We have deliberately avoided using the phrase 'his committee' despite its admirable brevity because we do not believe that such a phrase is compatible with the concept of a corporate approach; the officer is responsible to the Council for his actions, through the agency of the appropriate committee(s). It is in this area of informal contact between committee meetings that there is a need for a source of advice on the sensitive issues which inevitably arise in the course of day to day administration and which the officer must recognise as requiring member participation.

3.42 In some authorities special arrangements have been made to provide an immediate forum at which such issues can be discussed and decisions can be taken. One of these, Bradford CBC, has developed an extremely interesting system of 'Executive Groups' for this purpose and we reproduce an outline of how that system works at Appendix G. In doing so, we are well aware that to some people, both members and officers, the concept of executive groups within the Bradford Plan will be quite unacceptable and it is fair to say that, with one notable and not altogether surprising exception, we reacted initially in just that way. But we have since learned more about the system and, more important, have talked to both members and officers at Bradford about it and whilst it would be stretching the truth to suggest that there is no opposition to the system, we found that it enjoyed a great deal of support. In reproducing the scheme as part of our report we are not recommending the system as such; we are, in accordance with our terms of reference, merely inviting attention to its existence.

Briefing of chairmen

3.43 It is a traditional and generally accepted part of the officer's role to meet the chairman of committee before the committee meeting and brief him about the various items on the agenda. This facility is not normally extended to the 'shadow' chairman, but we have received evidence from some authorities in which the shadow chairman is also present at the briefing meeting. There are obvious political difficulties to be overcome, but we believe that there is much to be said in favour of such an approach.

3.44 Quite apart from that briefing meeting, a close relationship between chairmen of committees and the chief officers of the authority will go a long way towards the establishment of the atmosphere of mutual trust and respect to which we attach such importance. It is, however, at the actual committee meeting that the officer's professional knowledge and experience should play their major part in advising members. Ideally we believe that officers and committee members should be involved in a dialogue under the control of the chairman, so that members can really understand the implications of the decisions which they are being asked to take. It is at this point in the process that many decisions will be taken which will have a substantial impact upon the community and it is therefore essential that agendas should exclude all unnecessary matters in order to give adequate time for these decisions to be taken only after full examination and discussion.

3.45 A number of authorities and others submitting evidence to us have raised the question of advice from officers to party groups. This problem arises specifically when the central policy and resources committee, whatever its title, is a bi-partisan committee. In such circumstances the critical decisions are normally taken by the majority party group before the committee meets and their decisions are taken in the absence of and often without the benefit of advice from the officers. We believe that the advice of officers must be available wherever the effective decisions are taken and if it is the party group which makes these decisions then a way must be found of making the officers' advice available. This might be done through a representative group of majority party members, who would themselves be responsible for briefing the group meeting. It follows, in our view, that similar facilities should be afforded to the opposition party(ies).

Chapter 4

Fulfilling the member's role— organisational implications

The Council

4.1 The Council is the ultimate decision-making body within any local authority and by the very nature of the democratic institution which local government is, that role is one which must remain with the Council.

4.2 The way in which that role is exercised differs widely from authority to authority. At one extreme the full Council receives and considers copies of the minutes and reports of every committee meeting and the members in Council are at liberty to reserve any individual item for debate by the Council. In the centre are those authorities where the Council receives and considers reports in the form of summaries of the major activities of its various committees. As in the first example, members can then raise individual matters for debate, but, unlike the earlier example, they are limited to the major matters which are included in the reports. At the other extreme we have received evidence from an authority where virtually nothing comes before the full Council unless members specifically so require. In fact the difference between the two extremes is basically one of procedure, because in each case members receive all necessary information and select which issues they wish to be debated in Council. The difference lies in the process by which that selection is made.

4.3 Despite these variations, we have found that in many authorities the full Council is increasingly being regarded as a body whose major function, in terms of agenda content if not in importance, is to rubber-stamp decisions which have effectively been taken elsewhere, whether by officer, committee or party group. The result is that the proceedings of the full Council become more and more formal and ritualistic and its role is downgraded in the eyes of members, officers and, most important perhaps, the public.

4.4 The Council will usually wish to reserve to itself in the terms of delegation to committees the more important policy matters. In that case it will receive reports and recommendations from the committees on these reserved matters, with concurrent reports from the policy and resources committee where the latter considers it necessary. We believe that the Council should also have a role as a debating and policy-formulating forum. Debates on the broad policy options, perhaps on the basis of papers from committees of the sort issued from time to time by central government to stimulate discussion of particular issues, would enable the arguments on each side to be heard before effective decisions are taken. The press and public too would be better informed and, we believe, encouraged to play their part if they felt that important matters were to be debated before the effective decisions were taken.

The committee system

4.5 In our interim report (Appendix A) we urged the removal of all statutory requirements upon local authorities to appoint particular committees and although the Government did not wholly accept our recommendations, there will in future be more freedom for each local authority to set up the organisation which it feels will meet the needs of its own particular situation. We remain of the opinion that from a management point of view it is undesirable to require a local authority to appoint particular committees; doing so not only restricts the freedom of the authority to select an organisational structure for itself, but by creating 'statutory' and therefore 'special' committees for particular services it encourages both members and officers for those and other services to adopt a departmental rather than corporate approach.

4.6 The achievement of this corporate approach is perhaps the major task facing the new local authorities and although the opportunity for change presented by the reorganisation of local government will help, there will inevitably be substantial problems to be faced. Not the least of these will be the difficulty of welding into a team members from different authorities, each with his own traditions, practices and loyalties. It is at the level of the individual member that the seeds of corporate planning and management must be sown, for it is there that they must flourish. Corporate management is not something which is done behind closed doors in a policy committee meeting; it is a process involving every member and many officers.

4.7 Because the traditional committee system has been retained by the Government's decision in relation to certain services, we have not sought to find radical alternative systems of organisation at member level. What we have attempted to do is to bring more flexibility to the traditional system, without jeopardising its strengths.

4.8 Perhaps the first point to establish is that a change in structure does not necessarily result in a change in management process, though it may well facilitate such a change. To illustrate the point, we have received evidence from a number of authorities who have established a central policy committee, though it may be called a management committee or some other title. We have also had the opportunity of discussing the work of such committees with members and officers in the authorities which we have visited. In a number of authorities we have found that the so-called policy committee is in fact not concerned with the central policy and strategic decisions at all. In some cases it has become what one member called "the waste paper basket of the Council", operating as a low-key general purposes committee; in others it is responsible for any matter which comes up between meetings of other committees. What has happened in these authorities is that the structure has been changed, but the management process has not.

4.9 We have chosen to illustrate our point by reference to the policy committee; it is, therefore, logical that we should commence our discussion of structure from this central point.

4.10 In their evidence to us, the then Society of Clerks of the Peace of Counties and of Clerks of County Councils said:

"..... the authority tends to have a number of separate plans with separate programmes, and while there is normally some co-ordination of each of these programmes between the departments concerned, the authority does not have adequate opportunities of examining the programmes as a whole to decide whether they provide the best overall strategy".

4.11 This is a view which has also been supported by the findings of management consultants who have reported on the management and organisation of local authorities. For example, McKinsey and Co Inc concluded that one authority which they had studied:

"... in common with many other authorities, finds itself with an organisation and a system of making decisions that has changed little since the present structure of authorities was created out of the tangled web of local boards and functional administrations in the latter half of the 19th century. The democratic forms of Council and committee and the rigid hierarchical structure of the service have some great strengths but in many ways are not geared to the modern task of managing thousands of people and hundreds of millions of pounds of assets, nor to making complex often technical decisions on the development of those assets. The city has neither the organisation structure nor the planning system nor the management methods commensurate with the job".

4.12 We believe that these words apply with some force to all levels of local authority.

4.13 The two statements which we have quoted clearly imply the need for some form of overall plan towards which the authority will work and against which it can measure its achievements. There can be no improvement in the quality of the critical decisions regarding resource allocation unless there is in existence some yardstick against which priorities can be evaluated and competing claims can be resolved.

The Policy and Resources Committee

4.14 As we have already said, the Council is the ultimate decision-making body of the authority, and the broad policy decisions which themselves determine the overall plan for the community should be taken by the Council. In order to take those decisions the Council needs comprehensive and co-ordinated advice on the implications for the community and we believe that this function requires the creation of a central policy committee. Such a committee will aid the Council in setting its objectives and priorities and, once the major policy decisions have been taken, will be instrumental in co-ordinating and controlling the implementation of those decisions. It would have a

23

particular role to play in the formulation of the structure plan for the area, either directly in a county or by way of consultation in a district.

4.15 This 'Policy and Resources Committee' as we have chosen to call it, would, as its name implies, have ultimate responsibility under the Council for the major resources of the authority, finance, manpower and land (with which we include buildings). The central control of finance has long been accepted and we believe that the dual role of the policy and resources committee in advising the Council on future plans and objectives and in co-ordinating the implementation of those plans, necessitates overall control of the other major resources. It may be that in certain special circumstances, for example where a large central area redevelopment scheme is in progress, control over land and buildings should be delegated to the committee which has responsibility for the redevelopment programme, but we suggest that those occasions should be exceptional.

Resource sub-committees

4.16 In each of these areas of finance, manpower and land it is important that the policy and resources committee should deal only with matters of major importance, not, for example, with trivial questions of expenditure. The more routine matters requiring member participation should be dealt with by three resource sub-committees each dealing respectively with one of the three main resources.

4.17 The precise division of responsibility between the parent committee and its sub-committees is a matter which will have to be decided by each local authority, but in making that decision we would urge authorities to bear in mind that the parent committee has a vital strategic role to play. Unless there is strict control over its agenda it will become swamped with a mass of detailed items which will leave insufficient time for realistic debate and decision on the major issues.

4.18 The membership of the three resource sub-committees should not be limited to those who are members of the policy and resources committee. They will play a substantial part in the corporate management processes of the authority and thus provide an excellent oppor-

24

tunity for members to become familiar with and take part in the management of the authority as a whole. The presence of 'back bench' members will also go some way to counter any suggestion that all power is concentrated in the hands of the members of the policy and resources committee. For these reasons we recommend that a substantial proportion of members of the sub-committees should not be members of the parent committee. This form of organisation will enable members of operational committees to see and appreciate the need for a corporate approach towards the policy and resources of the authority. It is essential, however, that the chairmen of the sub-committees should be members of the main policy and resources committee.

4.19 If it is the responsibility of the policy and resources committee to control the broad allocation of the various resources of the Council, it must also have the overall authority to create the management and review processes which are necessary to ensure that those resources, once allocated, are properly used. For this purpose the committee will need to keep the organisation structure and management processes of the authority under continuous review and see that they keep pace with the demands made upon them.

Monitoring and review—The Performance Review Sub-Committee

4.20 As far as the review processes are concerned, the regular monitoring and review of programmes against defined objectives is a responsibility which must rest primarily on the members of the particular programme committee. That committee should ensure that its reviews are systematic and thorough and should satisfy itself that necessary action is taken to deal with any variation in or from the approved programme. We believe, however, that some form of independent review process should also be considered. What we have in mind is a body of members within each authority rather like the Public Accounts Committee. We believe that a watchdog body of this sort, with the standing and formal authority to make detailed investigation into any project, department, or area of activity would provide an extremely useful service to management. In our view that standing and authority is most likely to be derived from a close link with the policy and resources committee. The role of such a body, as we see it, is very much complementary to those of the resource sub-committees which we have recommended earlier and we suggest that it should in fact be a fourth sub-committee of that committee. It would therefore be chaired by a member of the parent committee. Other members need not be members of the parent committee, but would be called upon according to the knowledge, skills or experience which they could bring to bear upon the area being examined. They would include representatives of the appropriate committee. Service upon such a body would provide an excellent opportunity for the development and involvement of some of the younger members. We envisage that the "Performance Review Sub-Committee" would submit its report to the policy and resources committee and that the appropriate committee and department would have the opportunity to comment upon the report.

4.21 As we implied in paragraph 3.23, in its relationships with other committees the policy and resources committee is not the sole arbiter on all levels of policy and must not attempt to act as if it were. We would have preferred to find a title for the committee which would more accurately reflect the role which we have assigned to it, perhaps "Strategic Planning and Resources Committee" but as we have been unable to find a generally acceptable alternative we have retained the traditional 'Policy' title. In order to carry out the co-ordinating and monitoring role to which we have referred in an earlier paragraph, the committee should be able to comment on the reports of any other committee before they are submitted to the Council and should also indicate to other committees areas for review of policy or activity. On its own account it should be entitled to originate policy and make recommendations to Council within its own areas of specific responsibility, ie corporate planning, resources and management.

4.22 The detailed powers of the policy and resources committee will be a matter for each Council to decide, but we do emphasise the need to spell out clearly what its powers are; how far they are directory and how far advisory, and in what circumstances they are to be used. We believe that there are some matters which can most effectively be raised initially in the policy committee, for example major issues affecting the authority, particularly those which cut across programme or service areas, or issues where speed is essential and we recommend that the committee should as a matter of general rule have the power to deal with such matters. At Appendix H we set out suggested terms of reference which authorities may find helpful.

Membership of the Policy and Resources Committee

4.23 We have received a considerable amount of evidence about membership of the policy and resources committee. Broadly speaking there are two major issues:—

a) should the committee include members other than those of the majority party?

b) should membership be limited to, for example, chairmen of other committees?

4.24 It may well be argued that the first of these issues is not one upon which we should express a view and we recognise that this in particular is a matter which local political circumstances, rather than considerations of management, are likely to determine. Nevertheless, because of its impact upon management, and particularly communication processes, we believe that we should express an opinion.

4.25 The evidence which we have received is conflicting, with about as many in favour of a single party committee as against, irrespective of political party. In authorities which have single party policy committees, there is some evidence to suggest that the officers may be forced into putting forward arguments which in other authorities would be the responsibility of the opposition members. It is in such authorities that the minority party members often claim difficulty in obtaining information. At least one authority has abandoned a single party committee following a change of political power because of the mistrust of the committee which was generated when the successful party was in the minority.

4.26 The major disadvantage of a policy committee with minority party representation is, of course, that many of the effective decisions will be taken within the party group before the committee meets and this presents difficulties with regard to the giving of advice by the officers. In order to get over this difficulty, in one authority the majority party has set up a policy sub-committee on which the minority party is not represented and by this means the officers' advice is channelled to the party group.

4.27 On balance we favour minority party representation on the policy and resources committee; we believe that participation by the minority in the policy debates and decisions serves to ensure that different points of view are heard and more informed decisions arrived at. It also seems likely to lead to less of the sort of mistrust to which we referred in an earlier paragraph and may, in so doing, avoid some of the more violent reversals of policy which can occur following changes of power.

4.28 We have already commented on the need to recognise that members are qualified, both by aptitude and experience, to serve their authority in different ways, and we believe that it is particularly important to recognise this when considering questions of policy and resource allocation. Traditionally membership of the central policy and finance committee has been reserved for the chairmen of the service committees, plus, in some cases, a few other senior members, and there is a widespread feeling that the overriding qualification for membership of that committee is seniority. We accept that chairmen of major committees must sit on the policy and resources committee; indeed the evidence which we have received indicates that such a committee without committee chairmen has proved ineffective. We believe, however, that provision should be made for other suitable members to become members of the committee.

4.29 In at least one authority this is achieved by allowing the other committees to elect from their membership the appropriate number of members who, together with the chairman of the committee, will sit on the policy and resources committee. Subject to what we have said about opposition party representation on the committee, this appears to be an idea worthy of consideration by other authorities. Those members would not sit as representatives of their committee; they would have to take an objective view of the affairs of the authority.

4.30 In some authorities, members of the policy and resources committee are not members of any other committee and, although this effectively answers the complaint of members that all the power rests with the chairmen of committees, in practice it does not appear to work particularly well. We see no reason to exclude members of the policy and resources committee from other committee membership, with the single exception of the chairman of that committee. We believe that he should not be associated with any particular committee, though he should have access to the meetings of every committee, and may, as in some authorities, be an ex-officio member of each one.

28

4.31 Another matter on which we have received directly conflicting evidence is the question of whether the leader of the majority party should also be chairman of the policy and resources committee. In some authorities the view has been expressed that to combine the two roles results in too much power being in the hands of one person, but we consider that the policy and resources committee must, if it is to be effective, reflect the power structure of the majority party. It is inconceivable, in our view, that the party leader should not be a member of the committee and formally recognising him as chairman does no more than acknowledge that effectively he will lead the committee whether he holds that office or not.

Other Committees

4.32 In the years which have elapsed since the Maud Report, many authorities have reduced the overall number of committees. Some have done so in order to slim the administration and encourage co-ordination, some to reduce calls on officers' time, some to help break down departmentalism and others, we fear, merely because it was felt to be fashionable to do so. There can be no doubt that a large number of separate committees can present severe problems of co-ordination, particularly when those committees are linked not to the objectives of the Council but to the separate departments through which those objectives must be secured and we would not wish to disagree in any way with the Maud recommendation in this respect. But we do not subscribe to the view that, of itself, a reduction in the number of committees will cure all the ills of an ineffective management structure, any more than will the purchase of the latest gift-wrapped management package.

4.33 Although we are, by our terms of reference, required to advise on methods of improving management efficiency, it is at this point that we emphasise that in a democratic institution management efficiency cannot be the only consideration. It was put to us in evidence that our objective must be to make democracy as efficient as possible, not to make efficiency as democratic as possible and there is a good deal of truth in this.

4.34 Traditionally, elected members have served on a number of separate committees and have thus been involved in the affairs of the authority on a number of fronts. One immediate effect of any reduction in the number of committees is that either committees become larger or members sit on fewer of them. We have found little evidence to support the popular belief that members wish to spend less time in committee; indeed the most frequent complaint which we have heard from members is that where the number of committees has been reduced they have insufficient to do to satisfy them. It may well be that some potential members, particularly professional and business men, are, however, deterred from putting themselves forward for election because of the amount of time traditionally occupied by Council affairs. It is to be hoped that streamlining the structure and management processes will result in more of these potential candidates being willing to play an active part in local government but for this very reason it is to be expected that there will be opposition to such changes from some existing members.

4.35 Some authorities which have restructured their committees have, at the same time, reduced the size of each committee in order to improve its effectiveness. It is the combination of these two processes which brings sharply into focus the problem of providing each member with adequate opportunity to participate. It has been suggested to us that this situation will require local authorities to recognise that not all members will sit on a formal committee. Our enquiries and experience leave us in no doubt that local authorities are not ready to accept this and, although we hope that members will participate through less formal groups, we believe that at present only a structure which provides each member with a seat on at least one committee stands any chance of acceptance.

4.36 If our assumption is correct, there will have to be some compromise in terms of either the number or size of committees. Every formal committee carries with it a substantial workload in terms of preparation for meetings, attendance, minutes etc., and to create additional committees solely to meet the need for each member to have a committee seat would also be incompatible with our declared object of structuring the organisation to meet the objectives of the authority. It is therefore in relation to size that the necessary compromise must be made; whilst membership remains at present levels, committees may have to be larger than otherwise desirable.

4.37 If authorities are to have fewer committees there will be even

30

greater need than at present to exercise control over agendas. As much of the detailed work as can be shed should be taken up by delegation to officers, or, if member participation is necessary, to less formal groups of members. In order to keep the members informed about matters outside the responsibility of the committee(s) on which they sit, all committee agendas should be available to all members; with fewer committees this should present little difficulty. Members should be allowed to attend and, at the chairman's discretion, speak at meetings of other committees.

4.38 There is no 'best buy' when it comes to deciding the number of committees which a particular authority requires; the number will certainly vary between authorities and within limits is not critical, though basic management principles would suggest four rather than fourteen. There has, however, been wide acceptance of the Maud recommendation that the number of committees should be reduced and in general this has been achieved by grouping together certain linked services and by substantial delegation of executive powers to committees and to officers.

4.39 One particular authority, for example, has reduced its total number of committees from twenty-eight to twelve, another from twenty-three to ten, and a third from twenty-three to six and although reductions of this order must create transitional problems, not least in connection with the cut in the number of chairmanships and vice-chairmanships available to members, the evidence from the authorities concerned certainly supports the view that the overall effect has been for the benefit of both the authority and the community which it serves.

Grouping services and functions

4.40 Although there are wide variations in the actual groupings which have taken place, there are certain groups which have frequently emerged. One such is the merging of the various amenity services, under either an amenity services or recreation/leisure committee; another is the creation of a combined highways/planning committee. Prima facie these groupings seem both logical and reasonable and there is little doubt that they reduce the problem of co-ordination. But the evidence suggests to us that other groupings have sometimes been made on a rather superficial basis. The groupings require very careful consideration before they are formed and should be capable of being changed to meet changing local requirements.

Programme Areas

4.41 Some authorities who have submitted evidence to us have reorganised their committee system in the light of their overall plan for administering the work of the authority. After considering their main objectives, they have divided their work into spheres of activity, each with its own objectives and programme for meeting those objectives. Committees have been made responsible for each programme and for the allocation of resources within it. The results, of course, differ according to the circumstances of each authority. If we take the library service as an example, several authorities have included this with education in an Education (or Educational Services) Committee, whilst others are administering libraries through an Amenities and Recreation Committee. Another example is a protection programme area which includes both fire brigade and the consumer protection services (weights and measures etc). There is nothing to prevent one committee dealing successfully with these two apparently diverse services· if the idea of programme areas is accepted and we think that a more effective allocation of resources will result.

4.42 The advantage of building the committee structure on this basis is that it becomes directly linked to the main needs and objectives of the authority. It encourages a corporate rather than departmental approach so that each programme area committee can call upon and be serviced by the skills and experience of a number of different departments. The heads of the individual departments will, of course, have the right of direct access to the committee.

Area committees

4.43 With the increase in geographical area to be covered by individual authorities in many parts of the country following reorgani-

32

sation we have considered whether we should recommend the creation of area committees to be responsible for the administration particularly of county council functions within a defined area. We emphasise that in this section we are not discussing agency arrangements or the creation of advisory or consultative committees; what we have in mind are committees operating within a particular area under specific delegated powers from the Council.

4.44 It is, we suggest, beyond dispute that some services will require to be operated by officers on a local area basis and we have received a small amount of evidence which supports in addition the creation of area committees of the type and with the role which we have described in the preceding paragraph. Devon County Council, for example, have a number of area social services committees which have delegated to them—

"full executive responsibility for the running of the service within their area" subject to—

"compliance with the reserved matters and the expenditure not exceeding approved estimates".

4.45 Basildon Urban District Council, in a recent discussion paper "The New Counties—The Same or Different?"* in suggesting that integrated area offices will be required in the new counties, comprising sections of all appropriate departments of the county council, also state:

"At member level, control would be exercised through an Area Committee to provide for Councillor involvement in this method of organisation ..."

4.46 Notwithstanding these two papers, we have received no substantial body of evidence which supports the creation of area committees. A number of authorities have in fact abandoned this concept and we can see no advantage from the management or administration viewpoint. We accept unreservedly that the county councils in particular will have to consider methods of establishing and maintaining contact with the public in the areas in which they provide services and also, of course, with the district councils. It does not, however,

* *"The New Counties—The Same or Different?" Basildon UDC May 1972*

seem to us that this requires the setting up of area 'executive' committees with delegated powers.

Sub-committees

4.47 Generally speaking, the reductions which have taken place in the number of committees have been accompanied by a parallel reduction in the number of sub-committees and in the evidence submitted to us there has been a general view that a proliferation of sub-committees is undesirable. A sub-committee has a certain formal and legal standing and it may sometimes be necessary to create a formal sub-committee for this very reason, rather than make use of a less formal group of members. In general, however, we subscribe to the view expressed at the beginning of this paragraph; a standing sub-committee should be created only where there is a permanent job to be done and if created it should be given specific delegated powers within which to perform its task.

Functions of committees

4.48 Committees in local government are generally concerned with matters requiring decision and amongst the main criticisms of the present system are

(a) that the decisions with which they concern themselves are decisions which could equally or even more effectively be made outside the committee room and

(b) that because of pressure on agendas the time available for important decisions to be taken is wholly inadequate.

It is perhaps because of this situation that officers tend not to bring matters before committees until a decision is required, but we believe that it would be of great benefit if committees were able or indeed required to debate issues occasionally before the need for a formal decision arises, in much the same way that we have suggested the full Council should do.

4.49 We have already discussed the review function of the committee, but it is even more important that the committee should make a realistic and critical assessment of projects, particularly where alternatives are available, before irrevocable decisions are taken. It is very much a matter for the programme committee to decide

(a)   on the policy for the programme for which it is responsible;

(b)   on the means of achieving its objectives, taking account of the resources of money, manpower and, perhaps, land, which have been allocated.

It is specifically in these areas that the value of the non decision-making debate would, we believe, improve the understanding of the issues at stake and therefore, the basis of the final decision. This would be particularly useful in connection with the preparation of budgets for the ensuing year.

4.50 In some authorities it may well be possible or indeed preferable to hold such debates within the normal committee cycle, but a case can be made for separating them from the cycle if only to make it clear that they serve a different purpose. In suggesting this we do not have only the members in mind; there may well be a need to emphasise the point to officers as well.

4.51 In advocating the adoption of a 'programme' basis for committee structure, we have had as one of our objectives the breaking down of the departmentalism which thrives on the one-committee-one-department tradition of much of local government. We believe that programme committees which are serviced by several departments and disciplines will reduce the areas of friction and disagreement between committees which are evident in the departmental approach. There will inevitably remain, however, some matters which will cross committee boundaries and provision should therefore be made for joint working groups representative of all relevant committees to be set up as and when needed.

The role of the chairman

4.52 The office of chairman of a major committee is one of substantial influence within a local authority, though legally the chairman has no power himself to take decisions. The Local Government Bill maintains the previous situation in that it does not permit delegation to chairmen of committees, but it would be unrealistic not to recognise that despite this many day-to-day decisions have been and will continue to be effectively taken by chairmen.

4.53 It is, however, in his role as a link man with the policy and resources committee that the committee chairman is in our view most important, because it is through him that the essential lines of communication must flow. It is also the chairman who provides the vital link between the forward policy thinking of officers and the committee structure. A detailed analysis of the role of the committee chairman was incorporated in Volume 5 of the Maud Committee report and we do not intend to go over that ground again. We do, however, emphasise that despite the lack of any formal power of delegation to chairmen of committees the holders of that office exercise a great deal of influence over the running of the authority. It is therefore important that they should be chosen for their ability and not for other reasons.

Other groups of members

4.54 In addition to the executive groups which are an integral part of the system at, for example, Bradford and Haringey, we have received evidence of similar member groups either operating or contemplated in a number of other authorities. In one authority we were told that the problem of providing member participation following a streamlining of committee structure had been met by the setting up of a considerable number of such working groups. In the social services field, for example, there were groups concerned with fieldwork, welfare, and relations with the public and with voluntary societies. It seemed that these particular groups were performing a useful function, but in one authority many of the groups were so informal that the chief officers did not know they existed!

4.55 These groups take over one of the traditional roles of the chairman of the committee in that they provide an officer with an immediate point of reference at member level and enable him to sound out member opinion on action which he may be contemplating within the sphere of responsibility of the group. They also provide a means whereby individual members can identify themselves with particular areas of activity in which they may have a special interest; indeed some members may derive more satisfaction from their work on such a group than from their more formal committee work. We believe that such groups, which would not have the constraints of a formal subcommittee, have much to recommend them, both from the point· of view of organisational flexibility and member satisfaction.

The political element

4.56 The degree to which political influence is felt within a local authority varies from area to area, but it has become very clear to us that the whole management process can be very largely determined not only by the degree of political 'separation' between different parties represented on the Council but merely by the degree of political tradition in the particular area. In areas with a tradition of active political involvement the influence of the party group makes itself felt throughout the organisation. We found, for example, that even in an authority where 95% of the members belong to one political party, all effective decisions were taken by party group meetings before committee or Council meeting. The evidence which we have received suggests that the degree to which politics affects local government is likely to increase following reorganisation; some of the evidence welcomes this, some deplores it. We do no more than acknowledge the probable truth of the suggestion.

4.57 In 'political' authorities there will need to be a very close, though informal, working relationship between the majority party leader and the Chief Executive and in matters of management and organisation in particular we believe that there should be the opportunity for the minority party to express a view. A change in the management structure of an authority is not a matter to be undertaken lightly and though we recognise that the different political philosophies must have some impact upon the organisation, frequent structural changes made for purely political reasons can only result in a loss of both efficiency and morale.

Chapter 5

The organisation at officer level

Introduction

5.1   Both the evidence which we have received and the authorities which we have visited have emphasised the importance of local circumstances in determining the officer structure. We have seen, for example, authorities where specific organisational units have been created to deal with particular local problems and others where membership of a management group of Chief Officers has apparently been determined by the major policy programme of the Council. In theory the constitution of that group should change if there were a change in local priorities but whether it would in fact do so is a matter for speculation. Much, it seems to us, depends upon the local personalities, as well as local priorities.

5.2   Another authority illustrated the importance of local circumstances in a rather different way. The authority is relatively new with a Council largely composed of members without previous local government experience. Its organisation structure and management processes are in many ways the product of this situation; the members had no pre-conceived ideas about how the authority should function, with the result that the structure was very much determined by the ideas of the party leader working closely with the head of the officer service.

5.3   It may well be local personalities, at member or officer level, which will determine, for example, the degree of delegation which a Council is prepared to grant. We have seen authorities where there can be little doubt that the strength of personality of the leader coupled with those of the Chief Officers have resulted in massive delegation and the development of a strong Chief Officers' team. In another authority we found that Chief Officers had generally neither sought nor been given delegated authority. We believe that decisions should be taken at the lowest possible level commensurate with efficiency and responsibility and this puts a premium on officers of the right quality. It may well be argued that it also puts a premium on members and particularly leaders, of the right quality and we would not disagree with that. At officer level, however, the authority has the responsibility of selection; it has no control over the election of its own membership.

5.4 We have implied at an earlier point in this report that local authorities should build any new structures upon the existing professional base. Before developing our discussion of the departmental structure we should attempt to justify that view.

5.5 It is, in any event, a practical impossibility to do away with the essentially professional basis of local government organisation before the new authorities take up their full responsibilities on 1 April 1974, even if we felt that it was desirable to do so. Many able people have entered the professional ranks of local government in the knowledge and perhaps for the reason that the way to the top lies through the professions and this means that many of the best potential managers in the short and medium term are to be found already established in the professional ranks.

5.6 We have not, however, seen any evidence which would establish, or even suggest, that the professional basis of local government is of itself any worse than, for example, the generalist basis of the Civil Service. Both systems have their advantages, and both, when carried to extremes, their disadvantages and it is not without significance that at a time when local government is moving towards greater emphasis on management and a wider approach to its problems, the Civil Service is encouraging its generalist staff to adopt a more specialist (dare we say professional?) approach. Local government is and will remain responsible for a large number of executive services which will continue to require professional expertise; whether there will in the long term be a parallel development of wholly administrative skills on Civil Service lines remains to be seen.

5.7 Among the existing departments some are, by the nature of their function, more professionally oriented than others and in such departments most of the work is done by professionals in an environment which suits them. They derive satisfaction both from their own jobs and from the knowledge that there is a man at a senior level who both understands what they are doing and will speak for them. Although some of the newer professions are themselves products of local government, many of the skills required by local authorities are of general application and local government is competing for these skills with other employers. In order to continue to attract men and women of the right quality a worthwhile career pattern must be maintained and this means jobs at the top level available to the professional man.

5.8 This does not mean that there should not be any change in the traditional pattern of management; indeed we believe change to be essential on lines which we shall now develop.

The Chief Executive

5.9 The Maud Committee recommended that there should be one person recognised as the head of the authority's paid service who should have authority over the principal officers so far as this is necessary for the efficient management and execution of the authority's functions. We subscribe to this view. What his title should be is a matter for discussion and a number of possibilities have been suggested, including Clerk, Town or County Manager, Director General, Chief Executive (Officer), Principal Chief Officer and Principal City Officer. We cannot dictate what his title should be, but since some of those suggested have fairly definite implications about the job he is to perform, we should first decide what that job is to be. For the moment we propose to call him the Chief Executive.

5.10 The evidence which we have received suggests that there is very little support for an all-powerful Chief Executive; in fact only one submission advocated such an appointment. It is clear, however, that there is a great deal of room for discussion and argument about just what powers and authority he should have and many authorities have avoided the issue by not spelling them out. It would be all too easy to condemn this and, on the face of it, it leaves the Chief Executive in a very difficult position. But it is important to put the appointment into historical perspective.

5.11 Local government has been engaged over a considerable period in the provision of a number of separate services, each controlled by a separate department, with its own independent head of profession. This situation has developed strong professional motivation and loyalty to departments, but has resulted in certain basic weaknesses which are now being tackled by a number of authorities. In this traditional situation the 'primus inter pares' situation of the Clerk of the Council represents tacit acceptance of the fact that in such an organisation somebody has to exercise a co-ordinating role. What those same Chief Officers are now being asked to accept is, however, somebody who is not merely primus inter pares, but is definitively their superior and the fact that in many cases it is the same man as hitherto makes the pill more difficult to swallow. Attitudes cannot be changed overnight and the newly appointed Chief Executive has a critical human relations problem to solve if he is to become effective.

5.12 His first task is to gain the respect and esteem of his colleagues, because his true powers will come more from his own qualities and character than from anything written into his, or the Chief Officers' terms of appointment. We do not suggest that there should be no formal definition of his position vis à vis the Chief Officers, but it is, we believe, important to recognise both the difficulties and the limitations of spelling it out, particularly in any detail. There is much to be said for allowing the man himself to develop his own interpretation of the job within a fairly broad framework.

5.13 The range of issues and problems facing any local authority is too numerous and varied for the Chief Executive to grasp in detail and heads of departments must therefore retain the responsibility for the effective and efficient running of the services for which their departments are responsible. This means that the Chief Executive must act primarily as the leader of a team of Chief Officers and co-ordinator of activities. In that capacity he must ensure that the resources and organisation of the authority are utilised effectively towards the attainment of the authority's objectives. In addition he is the Council's principal adviser on matters of general policy and as first officer has a particular role to play as the Council's representative in contacts outside the authority.

5.14 We have received a number of descriptions of the role of the Chief Executive and at Appendix J we set out a suggested specification. This illustrates some of the many facets of his role, but does not clearly lead us to any particular title for the post. It has been put to us that since he has very little in the way of executive duties, the title of Chief Executive is misleading and that may be so, but no more so, we suggest, than Town Clerk. There are those who will favour retention of the latter title, but we believe that the Chief

Executive's role is quite different from that of the traditional Clerk and a new title is therefore required. The overwhelming volume of evidence on this subject has favoured either Chief Executive or Chief Executive Officer and we shall therefore use the former title in this report. In making their own decisions local authorities will no doubt give whatever weight they think fit to ours.

5.15 Having given some indication of what the job is and what we propose to call the man who is going to fill it, we must now consider where he is going to come from.

Background and Training

5.16 The majority of authorities which have appointed Chief Executives have in fact appointed former Clerks, either their own or somebody else's and such exceptions as there have been to this rule have generally been Treasurers. This might be expected to be a practice which would commend itself to a Group whose local government membership comprises members of those two professions, but we shall attempt to set aside our own prejudices and examine the situation dispassionately!

5.17 We believe that the selection of Clerks and to a lesser extent Treasurers to fill Chief Executive posts is a recognition of the need in this post for a man with 'across the board' experience. We do not believe that merely because a man is a lawyer or an accountant he is necessarily better qualified to be Chief Executive than, for example an engineer or an architect, but in the present local government organisation his experience of the authority as a whole does tend to give him an advantage over the man who has pursued his career in one of the other professional streams. The appointment of Chief Executive is a vital one for any authority and we believe that the field of selection should not be restricted to those holding particular professional qualifications, nor indeed to those holding any. The important thing is to get the best man for the job.

5.18 In order that local government as a whole can develop its future Chief Executives it must, we suggest, find a way of broadening the experience of officers within the existing professional ranks. For some professional officers loyalty to their profession is paramount and they would not wish to leave their profession for the rather less specific fields of management and administration even at the top level, but there must be others whose ambition and ability would fit them for such posts.

5.19 There is a strong belief among local government officers that this broadening can, in the local government context, only be done by management training courses coupled with experience on inter-disciplinary working groups. Mr. Woods, however, with his experience of career development in industry, believes that suitable young professional officers should be deliberately given experience of other departments as part of their grooming for management. He envisages a strong central personnel department which would be responsible for keeping an eye on such men and seeing that they were given the appropriate experience to fit them for the top posts. He recognises that this would mean that a man might be taken out of his professional career stream at a critical point in his career, but although opportunity for professional advancement could be reduced, he would have other chances in the general management field.

5.20 This sort of career pattern is, we gather, by no means unusual in industry and many of the top administrators and managers have initially come up a professional ladder. The Civil Service is now de-veloping an 'open' structure at senior levels and there have recently been appointments of professional officers to what have traditionally been senior administrative posts. All this suggests that this is something to which local government should give careful consideration, though we do not underestimate the change of attitudes which will be required nor the difficulties which are likely to be encountered. The men chosen for special treatment under such a scheme will, by definition, be the very best young men in the authority and the very fact that they are given the opportunity to broaden their experience will make them that much more attractive to other authorities with suitable vacancies. But this movement between authorities is something which has been a factor in local government management for a very long time and provides a very useful means of importing fresh ideas and impetus into departments. There is every reason for movement stimulated by development of the type proposed by Mr. Woods to operate to the advantage of local government as a whole.

5.21 We have been discussing the prospects of horizontal movement for the young professional officer, but we have also been asked to consider specifically the position of the administrator, whether qualified (eg DMA, DMS) or unqualified.

5.22 We have seen little general evidence of recruitment on a career basis of, for example, good quality general graduates of the type sought by the Civil Service for its former Administrative Class posts. One authority which did start such a scheme found that the wholly professional structure at senior levels effectively meant that there was no way of getting these young men beyond third tier level and has, we understand, now abandoned its graduate entry scheme. The Chief Executive of another large authority emphasised the need for high quality administrators at the top of the structure. He maintained that in his authority administrators were mobile between departments and had a future in senior management positions, but he also admitted that for an administrator there was no direct route to the top within his authority. It would be necessary for him to secure a top appointment in a smaller authority in order to 'by-pass' the unbridgeable gap caused by the wholly professional top structure and then use this as a stepping stone to top appointments in larger authorities.

5.23 On the other hand we understand that at least one authority is now contemplating starting such a scheme and clearly envisages that the careers of such graduates would be under central control and guidance. The intention behind that scheme is that these graduate administrators would move from department to department and should eventually have an equal claim for top management posts with those who come up the normal professional ladder.

5.24 We give examples of possible structures in Chapter 9 of our report and some of these make it possible for the general administrator to reach the top posts. Mr. Woods' suggestion for special treatment for selected young professionals would apply equally to any administrator who was thought to have the necessary qualities and he would compete on level terms with his professional colleagues.

Should the Chief Executive have a department?

5.25 This question really subdivides into two separate ones. First, does

44

the Chief Executive have direct line responsibility for one of the departments, particularly that formerly known as the Clerk's department, or if not, does he require a new department set up specifically to serve him?

5.26 The factual evidence of authorities which have appointed Chief Executives shows that a significant number continue to head the traditional Clerk's department and in some cases it is clear that the change of title does not reflect any real change of job. But this is not always the case; some Chief Executives who are by no means merely refurbished Town Clerks have told us that they feel it necessary to retain direct links with, for example, the servicing of committees, because it is only by so doing that they can be sure of keeping in touch with what is going on. We were told quite specifically of one instance where the committee clerks acted as the Chief Executive's eyes and ears and would report to him any moves by a head of department which they felt the Chief Executive might want to forestall. He could then take the necessary steps to nip such action in the bud.

5.27 It is true that the Chief Executive is likely to have a special relationship with the head of administration, as he will with the head of finance, but it does not, in our view, follow that he should have particular responsibility for either. We accept that he must have appropriate channels of information and can see that the committee clerks could form one such channel, though we would not wish to see them operating in quite the way described in the preceding paragraph. It seems to us, however, that if the Chief Executive has a department dealing, for example, with committee administration, he will also have departmental problems and responsibilities and for at least some of his time will be operating at the same level as other departmental heads. His staff will expect him to defend their interests in the case of inter-departmental conflict and it will be extremely difficult for him to rise above this role. A number of people have also told us that the creation of a 'boss' department can of itself make for difficulties. There is resentment of the superior status of its staff which is believed to arise not from the job they do but merely from the link with the Chief Executive.

5.28 It might well be thought that in the smaller district the Chief Executive should, for economic or other reasons, be responsible for one of the departments of the authority. We believe, however, that there is the same need for a detached Chief Executive to secure proper co-ordination and that there is great scope for him to exercise a wider co-ordinating, public relations and representative role than his counterpart in local government today finds possible. We therefore recommend that such district authorities should allow this role to develop by keeping their Chief Executives free of departmental responsibilities.

5.29 In some authorities where the Chief Executive is the titular head of administration it is his deputy who is effectively the head and in this situation we see no reason why the deputy should not be recognised as such and given the appropriate designation. We shall discuss the general question of deputies later in this chapter but it is appropriate to deal here with the specific question of Deputy Chief Executives.

5.30 We do not believe that there is any need for, or indeed much merit in, the creation of a separate full-time post of Deputy Chief Executive, in the way that, for example, Deputy Clerks or Deputy Education Officers are usually to be found today. We have already referred to the problem which a Chief Executive will face in establishing his relationships with his Chief Officers, and asking them to accept another man who, though possibly not senior to them in actual grading, would inevitably be closer to the 'centre', would only make it more difficult for them to accept the whole concept of a Chief Executive.

5.31 The corporate management concept suggests that each of the Chief Officers acts as the Chief Executive's deputy within his own particular sphere. If it is felt essential to designate one man to act formally for the Chief Executive in his absence, we suggest that this should be dealt with on an ad hoc basis by the Council. The important point which we wish to make, however, is that that designated officer is in no way removed from his role as Chief Officer by being so designated. His major function remains the management of his particular area of activity, but he will act formally for the Chief Executive in the latter's absence. It will be apparent from this that we would not expect designation to carry with it any automatic assumptions about succession to the Chief Executive's post.

5.32 Having concluded that the Chief Executive should not, in our view, be responsible for any of the general departmental functions, we have also considered the creation of a separate Chief Executive's department. We see difficulties in this idea too, particularly in the smaller authorities. The very nature and extent of the Chief Executive's job means that if his department is to do anything more than provide him with secretarial and personal services it will have to include a wide range of skills and experience and there is immediately a danger of duplicating the work done in the appropriate departments. Avoiding such duplication might involve removing skilled staff from those departments with consequent reduction in staff quality there and the beginnings of a vicious circle which could lead to ever increasing concentration of the quality work in the Chief Executive's department. This, we believe, would be to the detriment of the functions of, and services provided by, the other departments.

5.33 Whether the Chief Executive can actually operate totally alone is another question on which we have received conflicting answers. We have certainly seen some Chief Executives in large authorities who, apart perhaps from secretarial staff, have no staff working personally for them and they do not appear to find themselves in any way handicapped. On the other hand some Chief Executives who started off with no staff have either changed their views or are considering doing so.

5.34 It seems to us that there is much to be said for a Chief Executive having one or two personal aides working directly to him and this is a pattern which is beginning to emerge. In some cases the appointments have been made from outside the authority, but we believe that the creation of posts such as these provides an excellent opportunity for the development of suitable potential within the authority. We would like to see these posts filled on a limited term basis by officers of ability from any department as part of their general development. We envisage that suitable officers might be seconded for up to say two years in the knowledge that selection for such posts is itself a recognition of merit and a valuable stage in career development. This, of course, links closely with the ideas about career development to which we have already referred. In the smaller districts we accept that it may not be necessary for the Chief Executive to have aides of this sort.

5.35 A few authorities have approached this whole question of the Chief Executive in a different way. In this approach the Chief Executive has two deputies, each of whom is removed from the traditional responsibilities appropriate to his profession and together they form what is known as a triumvirate or troika. An example of such a system was found at Leeds where each member of the triumvirate carries overall responsibility for a group of services or departments, but the general management and control rests with the appropriate departmental head. We shall return to this in our next section where we discuss the subject of the Chief Officers management team, and also later when we consider departmental structure generally. As far as the Chief Executive is concerned, however, the triumvirate does mean that his total responsibility divides at a rather higher level than in the more traditional organisation and he has two deputies free from day to day management responsibilities. In the last analysis however, he is the man in control, and carries both authority and responsibility accordingly.

The Officers' Management Team

5.36 In an earlier paragraph we referred to the Chief Executive as the leader of a team and what we have in mind is essentially a small management team of Chief Officers. It is one of the main tasks of the Chief Executive to lead this team and to steer them towards common objectives. In the last resort, as our suggested specification in Appendix J makes clear, the Chief Executive has the necessary authority for this task.

5.37 The factual evidence which we have received from authorities indicates that in almost all of them there are periodic meetings of Chief Officers, but the role which such meetings play in the management of the affairs of the authority varies a great deal. In some authorities they appear to be convened mainly for the purpose of a collective consideration of the agenda for the next meeting of the Council; in others Chief Officers only meet together to discuss the occasional problem which affects them all. In each type of case there will almost certainly also be informal meetings between individual Chief Officers to co-ordinate the work of their departments.

5.38 We accept that such meetings have purpose and value, but they are of an entirely different nature from those which we have in mind and which are to be found in an increasing number of authorities. We believe that the officers' management team should have a corporate identity and a positive role to play in the corporate management of the authority. It is the counterpart, at officer level, of the policy and resources committee. Its members do not attend primarily as representatives of particular departments, though on occasion it will be necessary for them to speak in that capacity; they are there as members of a body created to aid the management of the authority as a whole. We were told by a Chief Officer from one authority that:—

"The formation of the Chief Officers group served to bring the officers together into regular consultation in a manner not previously known, with a resultant appreciation by one Chief Officer of the problems of the others and a greater awareness that each department was an element in the whole machine of the Council. It was as if departments which had hitherto regarded themselves almost as separate firms operated by a parent company found instead they were like departments in a department store, with a consequent increased knowledge of the work of the whole organisation".

5.39 A number of people have expressed the view that a professional Chief Officer is unable to make any valuable contribution to discussions on matters within the professional field of another Chief Officer and that the whole concept of a Chief Officers' team is therefore unlikely to succeed. Others have concluded that as some Chief Officers "had insufficient direct interest in a particular discussion" to warrant their being there, meetings should be confined to one subject and that only appropriate officers should be invited.

5.40 We disagree with these views. They suggest either that discussions are going to be so highly technical that only the man with appropriate professional training can take part, or that Chief Officers in local government are so blinkered by the confines of their particular professional field that they are unable to comment sensibly upon matters outside those immediate confines. We suggest that it is of the essence of the corporate approach to management that Chief Officers recognise that there are few if any major decisions which can be made in isolation without some impact upon others' areas of responsibility. Corporate management requires that the implications for the authority as a whole should be considered and discussed before decisions are taken. It may on occasions be necessary for a Chief Officer to subordinate his own particular interest to that of the authority as a whole. On another level each professional officer has a fund of knowledge and experience which is not only relevant to problems within his own field, but to the solving of problems of other fields as well and it is in the exchange of views and opinions within the management team that a true corporate spirit is likely to develop.

5.41 We have received evidence in support of our view. In one paper submitted to us it was stated that:

"All the Chief Officers .... should .... be expected to play the dual roles of professional and corporate team members";

in another that:

"the Chief Officer must recognise that he has duties outside his department in the furtherance of the corporate interests of his authority";

and in a third that:

" .... the members of the Management Board of Officers have each a duty to consider the affairs of the Council as a whole rather than their own particular departmental concerns .... there is very much to be gained by having opinions expressed by people of Chief Officer calibre on problems outside their immediate discipline".

5.42 The team's corporate identity should be recognised formally as part of the management structure and we would expect it to have a close relationship with the policy and resources committee from which it would receive instructions and to which it would submit corporate reports through the Chief Executive. Generally speaking we would expect such reports to be unanimous, but provision should be made for a strongly held minority view to be presented. The team should meet regularly and frequently, with a formal agenda. Because of the corporate nature of the team it has been suggested to us that all its members should attend meetings of the policy and resources committee. We see merit in this, but feel that this is a matter which must be left to each authority to decide. We envisage that the team would also be responsible for the preparation of plans and programmes in connection with the long term objectives of the Council, and for the general co-ordination, under the Chief Executive, of the implementation of those plans.

How large should the team be?

5.43 Broadly speaking the evidence suggests that there are two different approaches. One is that all Chief Officers (and in one district authority all deputies as well) are members of the team and the other requires some restriction in relation to the permanent membership. There are no hard and fast rules about this; much will depend on the size of the authority and the way its officer service is structured. One view put to us was that a team of nine is probably too large to operate with maximum efficiency. The evidence received, together with our own conclusions about possible structures, suggest that the team will probably number about six. Anticipating a little what we shall have to say about departmental structures in a later chapter, a team of six may well be large enough for all Chief Officers in the smaller districts to serve on the team, but in the larger authorities some traditional Chief Officers will not be permanent members. They would however normally be asked to attend if matters of specific concern to them were on the agenda and we therefore recommend that Chief Officers who are not members of the team should be kept informed of matters discussed by the team. If the management team's activities are not made known to those Chief Officers who are not members, distrust and suspicion are bound to be created.

5.44 In order to carry out the role outlined in paragraph 5.42, the management team in one authority has set up a series of inter-departmental working groups. The major group is the Corporate Planning Group, which comprises the deputies of all departments of the authority and which acts as a focal point on behalf of the management team. In addition it acts as a clearing house for reports coming to the management team from the other working groups. The work of the Corporate Planning Group includes the identification and review of objectives and priorities; the formulation of proposals for linking presentation of objectives, programmes and budgets and the monitoring of progress against plans.

5.45 Other working groups of the management team include a Research and Intelligence Group to determine data requirements and co-ordinate research, a Manpower and Management Services Group to "consider strategic questions concerning the acquisition, use, motivation, development and levels of the council's manpower resources" and a Lands Officers' group to monitor and co-ordinate the land acquisition programmes of the authority and consider matters of policy affecting the acquisition, holding and disposal of land and premises.

5.46 This list is not exhaustive, but serves to illustrate the involvement of the management team and its working groups in the central management processes of the authority.

5.47 Because the team is concerned with the totality of the functions of the authority, we find it difficult to lay down specific terms of reference. In a sense one could argue that anything and everything is within its overall responsibility and we do not wish to suggest that it should be restricted in any way. Its powers will be a matter for decision by each authority, but we suggest that it has two broad functions. The first is the long term strategic function of considering and advising on what policies the Council should be adopting to cope with changing needs and circumstances and the second the overall management co-ordinative and progress chasing role.

The Chief Officers

5.48 In the course of our deliberations we have from time to time found ourselves in difficulties over nomenclature; a management board, for example, is used to describe a body of either members or officers and a principal officer can mean anything from a director in charge of several departments, each headed by its own Chief Officer, to a third tier man in one of those departments. Up to now we have used the term 'Chief Officer' in what we hope will be understood as the traditional way, but in this and subsequent sections of our report we wish to distinguish, where appropriate, between those Chief Officers who are members of the management team and those who are not. We do this by designating the former Principal Chief Officers when it is necessary to make the distinction; the latter we continue to call Chief Officers. The traditional title of Chief Officer is one which has special meaning and status in local government and we see no good reason to deny its application to heads of individual departments. This means, of course, that we cannot use the familiar title of Chief Officers' Group and have therefore used the phrase Management Team to describe this body.

5.49 The top appointments to the new authorities will need to be settled as soon as possible and the increased responsibility of the Principal Chief Officers will require that the salary structures be sufficiently flexible to take account of this type of management structure.

Management ability

5.50 At an earlier point in this chapter we referred to the need for officers of the right quality and we now wish to develop this a little further. Most senior officers in local government have been appointed on the basis of their professional knowledge and ability and relatively little attention has been paid to management skills, which we suggest are at this level equally, if not more important. The officer's professional qualification qualifies him for the middle level jobs in his profession and it is at this level that he should get his basic managerial experience. From this point in his career his advancement should depend progressively more on his managerial ability and, as we have already suggested, his experience should be as widely based as possible in order to equip him for the most senior posts.

Selection and appointment

5.51 The appointment of all Principal Chief Officers and Chief Officers is, we accept, a member function. Selection at this level is a very responsible task and we would favour a nucleus of permanent members of a small selection panel of members from the policy and resources committee aided, as appropriate, by one or two members of the relevant programme committee(s).

Review of performance of Chief Officers

5.52 Much of the evidence which we have received has emphasised the question of accountability of Chief Officers and we stress the need for review of performance to be carried out on a systematic basis. At Principal Chief Officer and Chief Officer level we suggest that each officer should have an annual appraisal of his performance by, perhaps, the Performance Review Sub-Committee to which we have referred earlier. The committee should, in our view, be advised by the Chief Executive. This appraisal should be very much a two way discussion between the officer and the members, at which the officer should be given a clear indication of how he is seen to have performed his duties during the preceding year and given the opportunity to make comments and suggestions. For the Chief Executive we suggest a similar meeting with the policy and resources committee.

5.53 We have considered specifically the question of limited term contracts for the Chief Executive and the Chief Officers. This question has been highlighted by criticism from the leader of one authority of the fact that there is no ' golden handshake ' scheme in local government enabling an authority to release a senior officer whose level of performance is falling through no fault of his own, eg for reasons of indifferent health or failing powers. He suggested that if adequate powers were given to local authorities to give generous early retirement terms this would in many cases be to the advantage of both the authority and the officer concerned and this is a matter to which we also referred in our interim report. Given such powers and a systematic review and appraisal procedure we see little benefit to be gained from limited term contracts and the overwhelming majority of our expert advisers across the whole field of local government shared that view when we put the question to them.

5.54 As an integral part of any system of review and appraisal we believe that there is a need for some system of financial reward for exceptional performance. At present, salary scales within grades are relatively short and there is no way in which a man on the maximum of his scale can be given additional reward within that grade. We recognise that there are substantial difficulties in this sort of differential reward idea, but we recommend that it should be given careful consideration when any question of salary structures is under discussion.

5.55 We have, in this section, been discussing the appraisal and review of performance of the most senior officers, but similar processes must be built in to all levels of the authority's organisation in order that all members of staff may be aware of their senior officers' views of their performance.

Deputies

5.56 The tradition under which each Chief Officer has his own deputy is well established in local government, but is one of the traditions which is beginning to be questioned in some authorities. It is perhaps worth saying that, as a generalisation, it is in the authorities which have made the most sweeping management reorganisation that the deputy system has come under the severest attack. Some of the management consultants who have been active in the local government field have also come out firmly against deputies in a one-to-one relationship to their Chief Officers.

5.57 We put this general question to our expert advisers and the overwhelming response from them was in favour of retention of the system on a variety of grounds including the need to relieve the Chief Officer of the day-to-day management of the department and to provide a stand-in and known point of contact for members in the absence of the Chief Officer. Much emphasis was placed on the desire of elected members to have one person, rather than one of several, to whom to take their problems or complaints in the absence of the Chief Officer, but we do not regard this of itself as a particularly strong argument in favour of an additional tier of management within a department. Another argument in favour of a deputy in each department was that it provided an essential link between the various elements of the department and its head. We can see that in some departments the Chief Officer might have such a wide span of control that he needs a co-ordinating level of management, but a single deputy is in no better position to link the "various elements" than the single Chief Officer.

5.58 Although it seems to us that many of the arguments advanced in favour of departmental deputies would apply equally to deputies to directors of grouped services, our advisers were divided when considering this subject.

5.59 We do not believe that there is a need for every Chief Officer automatically to have a deputy, but accept that the nature and weight of the work of a Chief Officer may call for such a post in some cases. We suggest, however, that the justification for this post between the Chief Officer and the heads of the various sections of his department should be critically examined and that any such post should be kept under review.

Departmental structures

5.60 It is not our intention at this point in our report to go into specific detail about the organisation of departments to cover the functions allocated to the different types of authority. That is a matter we deal with in Chapter 9. What we want to do here is to consider the broad structure of departmental organisation within which those functions will be administered.

5.61 In Chapter 4, when dealing with the organisation at member level, we have suggested that the committee structure should be based on programme areas rather than the provision of specific services. Such programme areas may on occasions coincide with the amalgamated activities of various departments, but they will not always coincide exactly. We must therefore consider whether the departmental structure is to be based upon the same principle and therefore to coincide with the committee structure.

5.62 Although, in our view, programme areas represent a proper division of member activities, leading, one hopes, to some measure of achievement of the objectives of the authority, we do not consider that the same applies to the organisation of the services which implementation of those programmes will require. Many programmes will require the deployment of skills and knowledge which will go beyond the confines of any particular profession and a departmental structure founded upon programme areas would, therefore, be likely to involve the breaking up of the strong professional base of local government. It would also perpetuate the one department one committee link which has so fostered the development of departmentalism in the past. The Maud Committee recommendation for a substantial reduction in the number of committees has in many cases led to a parallel attempt to reduce the number of separate departments in order to maintain this direct link and in general this has been done by the creation of directorates.

5.63 The word 'directorate' is freely bandied about in discussions and articles about local government structures, but we have found that it has more than one meaning, or at least that directorates come in different guises. Much of the evidence which we have received has failed to make it clear which pattern of directorates it is discussing and we have therefore identified a number of different interpretations, each of which has at its root the grouping together of a number of separate departments, but which differ substantially in the management processes which result.

5.64 The first point which the evidence shows is that some authorities have established directorates right across the board, bringing every department into one or other of the directorates, whereas others have limited directorates to the 'line' departments, leaving the supporting services as separate individual departments. By way of example, one authority has directorates of

Technical Services
Engineering
Development and Town Planning
Housing and Community Services
Education
Social Services
Health
Finance
Administration

whereas another has directorates of

Engineering and basic services
Recreational services
Housing
Social Services
Health Services

and support services are provided by the

Clerk
Treasurer
Valuer and Estates Officer
Planning Officer
Architect

5.65 In addition to this basic difference in approach, however, there are very substantial differences in the concept of the directorate, particularly when it comes to determining the role of the director.

5.66 In a number of authorities it is clear that the director has a co-ordinating role only, and this is frequently the case where all departments are included in one or other of the directorates. Some officers and members who are operating a system in which the director does not have line responsibility for the component parts of his directorate have expressed reservations to us about the system. The criticisms fall broadly into three categories, as follows:—

a)   in order to bring every department into a directorate and to keep directorates more or less evenly balanced, some unusual, if not illogical groupings have to be made;

b)   the co-ordinating director is merely an additional level of management and in some cases is felt to be coming between the elected member and the Chief Officer responsible for a particular service;

c)   because of the illogical groupings, the director is asked to co-ordinate the functions of unrelated departments. The result is that it is the individual head of department rather than the director who remains the prime point of contact and the director's position is in danger of being undermined.

5.67 We have reservations about the 'co-ordinating director' system; the arguments against it seem to have considerable force and we have seen and received evidence of directorates which contain some very odd bedfellows. More important, perhaps, the people who are actually operating such systems appear to encounter practical difficulties.

5.68 An alternative interpretation, which is less common than the one we have just described, is that of the director who heads a totally integrated directorate and who has clear line responsibility for the services provided by the various divisions of his directorate. Such total integration is fairly rare; more often the director heads an organisation which consists of a number of separate units, each with its own clerical support, though he still has line responsibility for the various departments, or sections, of the directorate. The Director of Development and Town Planning in the first authority to which we referred in paragraph 5.64, for example, is responsible to his Chief Executive for "the effective management of architectural, town planning, development control, building inspection and estates and valuation services and for their efficient planning, organisation, direction and control". It is made quite clear that the heads of those departments report to and are responsible to him. If the director's responsibility is to be as clear cut as that, the subject matter of the various departments should be sufficiently cohesive to enable him to get a reasonable grasp of what is going on within his directorate as a whole.

5.69 One other pattern which we have seen, though not strictly a directorate system, is nevertheless worth mentioning. In this pattern the Principal Chief Officers have an additional representative role on the management team, though they have no line or even co-ordinative responsibility for the departments which they represent, and except in matters of technical/professional content they are expected to represent the views of their 'client' departments.

5.70 We have gained the impression that some groupings are easier to put into effect than others. We do not have in mind the problems of grouping dissimilar functions, though this, as we have pointed out, can cause difficulties. But the evidence suggests that, for example, the creation of a Technical Services Directorate, comprising, say, architecture, engineering, planning and valuation is far more likely to lead to internal conflict than the creation of a Directorate of Educational Services which covers, in addition to education, perhaps arts, museums, libraries and even recreation.

5.71 In part this is due to the general problem of relative status when merging departments which have previously been both independent and equal, (and this problem is highlighted when it comes to choosing the director!). It seems however to go deeper than that and to reflect the long standing rivalry which exists between some of the individual professions. We do not suggest that we have a simple answer; it is one of the problems which management in the new authorities will have to face if they adopt a directorate system.

5.72 We consider the merits of setting up particular directorates in the different authorities in Chapter 9 but one suggestion which has been put to us has application to all types of authority and it therefore seems appropriate to mention it during this general discussion of the subject of directorates. This is the concept of a Director of Resources, who would be responsible for the management of the authority's resources of land, finance and manpower. In this role a director would have a very close working relationship with the policy and resources committee and there would, we suggest, be great difficulty in defining his role vis à vis the Chief Executive and the management team. In one sense the Chief Executive himself acts as Director of Resources and we do not believe that a separate director would be a workable arrangement.

5.73 To sum up, we believe that the concept of a director responsible for a number of departments which have been integrated may lead to improved co-ordination and communication between those departments, but we have reservations about directors who are merely co-ordinators of independent functions. There is little point, in our view, in forcing efficiently run departments into illogical groupings merely to provide an even balance of work between one director and another. Some departments, particularly those with a 'staff' rather than a 'line' function may well be more effective if left alone under their own Chief Officer. If, in the result, one is left with directors whose work load and/ or responsibility is unequal, this difference must be recognised in terms of status and salary.

Relationship to committee structure

5.74 As a general rule we do not believe that it is necessary, or even desirable, for the committee and departmental structures to coincide. Some authorities who have maintained this direct link are now facing problems of ' super-departmentalism '; the attempt to cure the patient of one malady appears to have resulted in a different, possibly more virulent, complaint.

5.75 If the committee and departmental structure are not going to coincide in the old way, then some subsidiary organisation has to be created in order that committees receive the services which they require. In some cases, of course, there will be one department which will still clearly serve one committee, but in others it should be the responsibility of the Chief Executive and the management team to set up the necessary inter-disciplinary working groups to serve the programme committees, or more accurately perhaps, to ensure that such groups are set up. We envisage that each group will be under the control of a senior officer appointed from a discipline appropriate to the task for which the group is conceived. It will be possible, by use of such groups, to bring all the necessary professional skills together into a unified team with a defined objective.

5.76 This combination of the traditional 'vertical' structure and the 'horizontal' inter-disciplinary working group is known as a matrix form of organisation. This type of structure can operate both through programme teams giving advice and service to committees concerned with the general administration of particular programmes, or at the more detailed level of execution through teams working on specific projects. The membership of teams at either level can be amended or supplemented, new teams can be set up and existing ones disbanded as circumstances require. Herein lies one of the great advantages of this matrix system of management. By its nature it is flexible and adaptive, unlike the rigid bureaucracy which we suggest that it should replace. It provides excellent opportunity for suitable officers at second, third and fourth tier to head programme or project groups and gain first hand experience of management in a multi-disciplinary environment.

5.77 Although many authorities are making increasing use of multi-disciplinary working groups for specific projects, few, if any, have gone as far as we now suggest. Coventry CBC are probably as far along this particular road as anybody and we found an impressive sense of commitment and enthusiasm there which contrasted sharply with the very mixed feelings in some of the other authorities which had undertaken substantial changes in management structures.

Area organisation at officer level

5.78 With the creation of local government units covering larger areas, there will, we believe, be a need in many authorities, not only at county level, for a local office organisation, particularly in relation to services which have direct contact with members of the public. This is a matter which we have been asked to look at particularly and is one of the questions upon which we consulted our expert advisers.

5.79 Emerging from their comments are three main reasons for area offices, viz:

    (i) to bring services to the place of need;

(ii)   to provide a point of ready public access to the (county) organisation;

(iii) to properly deploy resources of staff, plant and equipment and materials.

5.80 We have given particular consideration to the location of the county area office in relation to the offices of the district council and we believe that there is a strong case to be made for having both within the same building. To the man in the street it is often relatively unimportant which particular authority is responsible for the service which he wishes to contact and indeed the use of the powers in the Bill relating to the discharge of functions may make it more difficult for him to decide to which authority he should go. If both authorities have representatives in the one place he may need to be redirected from one room to another, but is less likely to suffer the frustration of being passed from one organisation to another. We realise that in many cases district council offices may be scattered in different buildings and in those circumstances we suggest that the local county office should be within the main or headquarters building, thus creating an effective civic centre, which might well make use of common services provided by the district council.

5.81 The next question which we considered was whether the ' areas ' for the county services should coincide with the boundaries of the new districts, either directly, or in such a 'way that they comprise either multiples of or defined portions of those districts. In order to make the most effective use of the combined arrangements described in the preceding paragraph we believe that this should be the aim wherever possible.

5.82 We believe that area offices should operate under clearly defined delegated powers. County services within the area will need to be co-ordinated both between themselves and with the district services and this may warrant the appointment of an administrator or co-ordinator who would be responsible to the management team and the Chief Executive for the efficient management and co-ordination of the local county organisation. Because it will, in many cases, be at the local office that the face to face contact with the public will be made, authorities should ensure that the staff there are of high quality. Posts in local offices should not be regarded as second grade jobs, to be filled only by those with insufficient drive or quality to cope with head office work.

Chapter 6

Personnel management

Introduction

6.1   Our terms of reference require us to pay particular attention to "internal arrangements bearing on efficiency in the use of manpower". We take this phrase to mean something more than the extension of the existing processes for examination of claims for additional staff.

6.2   Local government is highly labour-intensive, frequently being the largest employer within its area and generally speaking there is relatively little scope for improvements in efficiency and effectiveness through investment in new plant and equipment. Such improvements must therefore come through more effective use of the human resources of the authority and the provision of suitable management structures is not, of itself, sufficient to ensure effective performance by those operating within those structures.

6.3   In view of its labour-intensive nature it is surprising to find that, by comparison both with industry and other areas of the public service, local government appears to lag behind in its recognition and development of the personnel management function. We have become convinced during our deliberations that it is an area of management which has not hitherto been given sufficient recognition in local government. The manpower resource, above almost any other, is costly, inevitably wasting, capricious in behaviour and capable of development and our decision to devote one chapter of our report to the subject of personnel management may be taken as an indication of the importance which we attach to it.

The present position

6.4   "Establishment Man" is a species well known not only in local government, but in other parts of the public service. Essentially he is believed to have two main functions; the first to control the day to day administration of rules about pay, conditions of service etc, and the second to act as the Council's watchdog (some would put it a good deal more forcibly) in respect of staffing claims by committees and heads of departments. In some cases it may also be his job to assist with disciplinary matters.

6.5   In a great many authorities the establishment officer is also in charge of the management services unit and this further emphasises the 'control' side of the function. With the increasing use of work study and O and M techniques some authorities have created separate management services units, but these are still closely linked with the establishment officer's responsibility for control over staff numbers.

6.6   This rather narrow view of the role of the establishment officer in local government has become widely accepted not only within the local government service, but also outside it. Because it is believed that the only reason for his appointment is to perform the functions outlined in paragraph 6.4, the establishment officer has had but little opportunity to widen his role; he has in effect become a prisoner of the role which he has been given. The result is that men qualified in, or at least having an interest in the wider aspects of personnel management have in some areas been deterred from applying for posts within local government establishment sections and this too has prevented the development of the personnel management function itself. In the professionally oriented world of local government, the non-professional establishment function has offered little to the young man with a Chief Officer's ballpoint in his briefcase.

Personnel management elsewhere

6.7   In industry enlightened companies have long regarded personnel management as a matter of quite basic importance to the efficiency of the organisation and the senior personnel manager is often recognised as a man with a voice on the main policy-making body. The same can be said for many areas of the public service.

6.8   We were able to discuss the role of personnel management

64

with the personnel manager of a large industrial enterprise. In that company, personnel management is seen as a positive function which has among its aims:—

a) to promote the effectiveness of human resources both in the short and the long term;

b) to create and maintain a climate in which changes which are to the advantage of the company can be achieved.

6.9 Some of the methods involved in improving the effectiveness of staff can be found in local government; we have in mind for example, manpower planning, including the examination of future requirements and the consequences of implementing particular alternative manpower policies. Some authorities are also paying considerable attention to such matters as the importance of recruitment advertising and the general effectiveness of recruitment methods. Other matters with which the personnel manager is involved have in our experience, however, rarely been developed in local government, though they are included in the syllabus of many management courses. In how many local authorities could one find, for example, a positive approach to the improvement of the quality of jobs, or the training of senior staff and members in selection techniques and interviewing skills? In how many authorities is there anybody who can advise on the effect of organisational changes upon employees and how managers should be trained to manage change? What impact have past organisational changes had upon wastage rates? Who are the high flyers within the authority, not only amongst the professional staff, but amongst the younger administrators? What training needs do they have? How should those needs be met? What is the authority's policy on career development for such people? The list of questions is almost endless, but all fall squarely within the remit of the personnel manager in industry. Our experience suggests that there are very few local authorities where the personnel function has been developed sufficiently to answer them.

6.10 The personnel manager in industry is also likely to be concerned with the whole field of industrial relations. It is his responsibility to represent the company in consultations and negotiations with the trade unions and a great deal depends on his skill and ability in this field.

6.11 In the Civil Service too there is increasing emphasis on the importance of personnel management. The Fulton Report on the Civil Service was critical of personnel management within the Service and recommended that the responsibilities of staff engaged in personnel work should be enlarged and their status improved. Sir William Armstrong, Head of the Civil Service, in a speech at a recent conference of the Institute of Personnel Management said:—

"Personnel administration is important, but it is basically a negative function and the old personnel administrator saw his job in terms of recruiting people to fill vacancies, paying them, applying the rules to them and dealing ad hoc with any problems which arose. But personnel management is very much more than this; an altogether more positive demanding job.
It is not surprising that the Civil Service, with a highly developed and structured personnel administration system, was in some ways slow to respond to this change of emphasis. The change of climate was given a considerable impetus by the Fulton Committee's report ... since then "Establishments Man" has gradually been giving way to the personnel manager".

6.12 This change is reflected in the structure of establishment divisions within government departments. The Department of the Environment, for example, has a separate Director of Personnel Management in addition to other Directors responsible for inter alia, management services and establishment control. These directorates which are each at Under Secretary level, come together under the Director General of Organisation and Establishment, a Deputy Secretary. The Director General is a member of the Department's Management Board.

6.13 The Commission on Industrial Relations, in its Second General Report (Command 4803) emphasised the

"... need to ensure that in the formulation of company policy, industrial relations implications were considered from the outset. For these reasons, we have stressed the need for adequate staff resources to be allocated to industrial relations work and the advantages of assigning the responsibility for personnel and industrial relations work to a particular board member as a major or sole responsibility".

The Commission also reported that one particular company

"... was advised to strengthen and reorganise its personnel department, which should be represented at the highest level in the company's executive structure by an officer whose sole responsibilities were for personnel and industrial relations matters".

6.14 The human problems of management in local government are in no way different from those in industry or the Civil Service. The resources devoted to the solution, and more important, the prevention of those problems in local government are in our view generally inadequate.

What is being done to improve the situation?

6.15 We did not when seeking written evidence specifically ask for information about personnel management, and the factual evidence which we have received is therefore somewhat limited. We have received some evidence to suggest that local authorities are beginning to accept the need for the preparation of manpower plans as part of the general forward planning process. A few authorities have introduced formal manpower budgets which force line management to take a realistic look at the manpower implications of their capital programmes, but these budgets, by their nature, concentrate on the 'demand' side of the problem. There appears to be little attempt to examine in any systematic way the 'supply' problem.

6.16 Stockport CBC have created a post of Chief Personnel Adviser, accountable to the Director of Administration and responsible for industrial relations, manpower planning and budgeting, remuneration, management development, training, recruitment and job evaluation. The post has only been filled for a matter of months and it is therefore too early to evaluate the impact which it is making upon the authority. Surrey CC have made a similar appointment, though with a different title, and we believe that a few other authorities are contemplating such appointments. In the context of some 1,400 local authorities, they are, however, very much the exception.

6.17 Some of those submitting evidence to us on the use and limitations of management services have suggested that personnel management should be integrated with management services; others have suggested with equal force that the two should be separate. The arguments put to us in favour of integration are that both functions contribute to the most effective use of manpower and often make use of common techniques. The Local Government Training Board, arguing against integration, maintains that management services are primarily problem solving techniques, whereas personnel management should be concerned with the development of policies and forecasting requirements. Mr. Raymond Nottage, Director of the Royal Institute of Public Administration, suggested to us that personnel management is a corpus of important work in its own right, whereas management services comprise a number of heterogeneous activities. Several consultants have also taken the view that the two functions should be separate, though some have suggested that they should report to the same senior officer.

6.18 We have received particularly useful evidence on this subject from Surrey County Council where the two functions previously combined at about third tier level have now been separated. There was a need to develop both functions and it was felt that, with the emergence of a number of specialised skills, the combined role would be too onerous for any one officer. The separation took place about two years ago and Mr. W. Ruff, the Clerk to the County Council, informed us that this—

"... enabled both personnel work and management services to receive higher priority within the organisation than before. On many matters there needs to be close co-operation between the two functions. Under Surrey's organisation there is indeed close coordination but at the very highest level (by the Clerk) and it has been very valuable to him and to the Council to feel that they are advised from both the management services and the personnel points of view".

6.19 We share this view that the two functions should at the operational level be separate wherever the size of the authority permits, with coordination exercised at a high level.

A 'new look' for personnel management in local government

6.20 The Local Government Training Board has recently published a report on training for staff engaged in personnel work* which includes a list showing the functions included in the work of establishment sections. This list, compiled from the results of a questionnaire issued to appropriate staff, shows that establishment control is one of the two most important functions at the present time.

6.21 This, of course, reflects the widely held view of establishments work to which we have already referred. So well 'established' is this view that any attempt to develop the wider role which we believe to be so important is likely to be severely handicapped by the mere use of the traditional title. We therefore suggest that local government should adopt the more widely recognised title 'personnel management'; this will more accurately reflect the function which we believe that the department should perform and is also more likely to attract suitably qualified staff.

6.22 Mr. J. K. Boynton, Chairman of the Working Party which produced the LGTB report to which we have referred, said in his foreword that the Working Party's recommendations—

"... will, however, only be of value to an authority that has first thought about the way in which the ... personnel function should be handled in a local authority. If an authority has not recognised that there is a personnel function, and has not examined carefully its effectiveness, then it would be unlikely to see the need to implement the suggestions in this paper".

6.23 In preparing this report we have as a general principle directed our comments to matters which affect the total organisation structure of the local authority; we have not looked in detail at particular departments within the authority. For this reason we do not propose to examine in detail all the functions and organisation of a personnel department, but it may be helpful to list the areas which we suggest should be within its responsibility. We can then look more closely at one or two specific items.

6.24 We were told in evidence to us that the Institute of Personnel Management had suggested the following definition of personnel

* *"Staff Engaged in Personnel Work"—Training Recommendation 8*

management:—

"Personnel management is concerned with the development and application of policies governing:

Manpower planning, recruitment, selection, placement and termination;

education and training; career development;

terms of employment, methods and standards of remuneration;

working conditions and employee services;

formal and informal communications and consultation both through the representatives of employers and employees and at all levels throughout the enterprise;

negotiation and application of agreements on wages and working conditions; procedures for the avoidance and settlement of disputes;

the human and social implications of change in internal organisation and methods of working, and of economic and social changes in the community".

6.25 On recruitment and selection we believe that there is a real need to examine the traditional processes of selection. The importance of the selection decision requires that local authorities should keep abreast of developing techniques; more attention should be paid to the design of man and job specifications; application forms should be designed to provide the maximum information relevant to the post to which they relate; interviewing skills should be developed and expanded. The qualified personnel officer may well have a particular role to play as a consultant to line departments in this field.

6.26 Education and training and career development can at best be unsystematic without a well developed system of staff appraisal. The development of training policies requires the identification of training needs, knowledge of training theory and practice, and skill in the actual training process. Professional training will normally be a matter which is well looked after by the appropriate professional body, but this will not be the case with the administrative, clerical or manual staff nor will it provide the individual training which management may wish to give to officers selected for special advancement. As far as career development is concerned we suggest that local authorities should adopt a more positive approach to the development of the potential of members of their staff as individuals. As part of this process we believe that there should be regular secondments of staff between different types of local authority, as well as between local authorities and industry or the Civil Service. In addition to broadening and developing the individuals concerned, such a system of exchanges would lead to better understanding of the problems which face others. We are not unmindful of the practical difficulties but in view of the benefits to be derived they should be faced and overcome.

6.27 We have referred earlier to the relative lack of attention to the 'supply' side of manpower planning. An effective staff assessment system is an essential requirement for this purpose, as it is for the development of any system of promotion which is, and, equally important, is seen to be based on merit.

6.28 In the industrial relations field we believe that it is the personnel officer who should be the expert in the design of appropriate procedures and systems of communication with representatives of the staff. He himself should be the recognised channel of communication between the Council and the trade unions on matters of manpower and industrial relations policy, and he should also advise line managers on the conduct of negotiations on the more 'domestic' issues which are properly their concern. Such an arrangement would ensure consistency and continuity of industrial relations policy and would also ensure that management at the centre was aware of the general industrial relations climate throughout the organisation. We do not suggest that the personnel department will be the sole repository of all the knowledge and information necessary to discuss and negotiate with the trade unions and staff associations on all matters concerning their members. The Personnel Officer will nevertheless have a particular responsibility to develop an atmosphere of mutual trust and confidence between the authority and its employees.

6.29 At the time of a total reorganisation of the kind facing local government as we write this report, the need for an understanding of "human and social implications of change in internal organisation" could hardly be overemphasised. For this reason the appointment of the head of the personnel department should be made by the new authority as soon as possible after that of the Chief Executive.

6.30 We have commented upon four major areas of personnel management work where we believe that there is need for substantial development in local authorities generally. We find support for our views in the LGTB report (paragraph 53) where, in a list of their own training needs identified by staff at present employed in personnel work in local government, all four are listed as areas in which further training is needed.

6.31 In the local government context the significant omission from the definition in paragraph 6.24 is manpower control. It has been suggested to us in one piece of evidence that this 'control' function should be separate from the personnel management function on the grounds that the need for additional staff is primarily to be justified by management, with advice available from management services. According to this view personnel management's role is primarily to fill the authorised complement of posts with staff of suitable quality.

6.32 Most of the evidence, however, does not support this view. The exercise of central control over staffing numbers is well established in local government and we have doubts whether it can be effectively substituted by departmental control. In the commercial field the profit element gives a ready and effective measure against which staff numbers can be judged, but without that measure, some central control seems essential.

6.33 In this 'control' area, the Personnel Officer is not only concerned with the individual claims for additional staff by the line departments. The ratios of technical to professional staff, non-operational to operational, headquarters to 'field' staff, are all aspects of control which require monitoring and examination. Manpower planning data, in terms of cost as well as numbers, will help to establish trends and expose issues upon which it is the Personnel Officer's responsibility to advise the Chief Executive and the Council.

Relations with other departments

6.34 If personnel management is to develop in the way we recommend, the status of the head of the department will need to be improved from that which he occupies at present in the majority of authorities. We recommend that he should have access to the Chief Executive and not be subordinated to the Director of Administration or any other Chief Officer. There is a possible danger in this proposal that the Personnel Officer will become 'judge in his own cause' so far as his own staffing claims are concerned. This is not our intention. His proposals will need to be critically examined by the management team, undertaking the personnel role themselves on such occasions. Indeed, authorities should ensure that the activities of the personnel department are subject to the same scrutiny as regards cost effectiveness as other departments. We do not suggest that at this stage the Personnel Officer should necessarily be a permanent member of the management team, though it is possible that the function will develop in such a way as to make this desirable at some future point in time. He should, however, frequently be called in to advise the management team on the personnel management implications of proposals under discussion.

6.35 Like management generally, personnel management is not an end in itself. Its objective is to influence and create an environment in which the authority can recruit and develop the employees it needs to achieve its objectives. It follows that although it has some executive functions in relation to, for example, salary administration, its major role will be advisory. Quoting again from the LGTB report:

"... managers ... are entitled to expect the advice and support of specialists in personnel work within their authorities, in precisely the same way as they have specialist support in other matters".

6.36 Chief Officers in other departments will normally be expected to accept and act on the advice of the personnel department on matters within the latter's specialised knowledge in exactly the same way as they would normally accept the Treasurer's advice on financial matters. Responsibility for day to day personnel management within departments rests firmly with the appropriate Chief Officer. The Chief Executive will expect the head of the personnel department to be responsible for seeing that the overall policies laid down by the Council are implemented.

6.37 The Personnel Officer's task is to get positive personnel policies in operation across the whole of the authority's staff. We suggest particularly that education and other services which traditionally have been largely independent of the central organisation should look to the personnel department for advice and assistance on personnel management matters.

6.38 In this discussion of personnel management as a function which is central to the local authority's work and activities as a whole we have inevitably concentrated upon its place in the overall management structure of the new authorities. It should, however, be recognised that some departments in the larger authorities will contain substantial numbers of staff and many of these will, we suggest, justify the appointment of departmental personnel officers. The calibre of staff employed at the departmental level must also be high. They will work closely with those in the central unit sharing a common professional approach and will be under the Chief Personnel Officer's guidance and direction in professional matters.

Staffing the department

6.39 In arguing as we do for a recognition of the fundamental importance of the personnel management function in the new authorities, we do not suggest that the effectiveness of the new department should be measured by weight of numbers. Adequate staff resources are essential, but the influence and contribution of the department will depend above all upon the status, authority and respect for its advice which the authority is seen to give it and upon the quality of the staff which it employs.

6.40 The indications are that there are at present relatively few staff within local government who are adequately qualified for the personnel management function as we envisage it should be undertaken. This is not intended as a criticism either of establishment officers or of their staff; most of them have not been required to undertake the necessary studies, nor have they had much opportunity or even incentive to acquire relevant experience. This is a situation which there is still time to do something about before reorganisation takes place and we strongly recommend that existing authorities should see that the necessary training is commenced immediately. In particular we suggest that authorities should contemplate the secondment of appropriate senior personnel staff to industry or other areas of the public service where the function is well developed.

6.41 In addition authorities should consider as a matter of urgency the recruitment not only of suitably qualified staff but also those with the necessary potential. The capacity and attitudes for personnel management do not derive from any one academic discipline. Our information is that graduates are often recruited by industry for personnel management, but the right personality is more important than academic background. The new local authorities will need personnel managers of high quality if the human problems of re-organisation are to be overcome.

Chapter 7

Other central functions

Management services—The meaning of the term within local government

7.1   The management services function in local government has assumed increasing importance and status in recent years and many authorities have set up management services units headed by an appropriately designated senior officer. Some of these units include the establishment and personnel function; indeed in some cases this is the primary role and a number of those who responded to our request for evidence on the use and limitations of management services dealt mainly with the need for an improvement in personnel management. For the reasons which we have given in the preceding chapter we believe that personnel management and management services should be separate, and we therefore propose in this part of our report to exclude the former from our discussion of management services.

7.2   Broadly speaking we have received two categories of evidence on this, as well as other matters. Firstly we obtained evidence which might be termed 'opinion' evidence from various sources and secondly 'factual' evidence from existing local authorities supplemented by comment. In the field of management services there was substantial agreement between the 'opinion' of what constitutes management services and the 'fact' of what is actually happening on the ground.

7.3   The evidence submitted contained such comments as:

"The one management service in use by the Council is work study"

"The Council has a substantial Management Services staff (engaged in) Work Study and O and M"

and, most definitive of all

"Management services, ie O and M and Work Study ..."

Overall it was only O and M and Work Study which commanded anything like general acceptance as functions of management services units; other skills and techniques achieved no more than occasional references, and it is clear that in many authorities the phrase "management services" is synonymous with O and M and work study only.

7.4 A recent editorial in Local Government Finance* stated:

'Starting with O and M one has seen a considerable plethora of various techniques and aids being suggested and/or introduced over the last two decades. These have ranged from work study (with or without incentive bonus schemes) to operational research, network analysis, computers, management accounting, CBA, management by objectives, DCF and of course PPBS."

7.5 This is an impressive list, and is complementary to the evidence which we received from the Society of Town Clerks that:

"The term 'Management Services' comprises all those services which help management to plan, control and improve the activities of the organisation in a general sense. The term is wider than the orthodox interpretation which is generally limited to efficiency and productivity services."

7.6 In the light of these comments the very title Management Services Unit is perhaps misleading if only O and M and work study are covered.

Work Study

7.7 As far as work study is concerned, we do not believe that a large central unit is necessary. Work study practitioners will operate within individual departments and should be under the day to day control of the line manager. We suggest that there is, nevertheless, a need for a relatively small central unit to control the overall deployment of work study staff in the interests of the authority as a whole, and to ensure that new techniques are evaluated and staff trained in their use. It is through this central unit that line managers would obtain the services of work study staff for their departments. The unit would also be responsible for setting up work study teams to undertake any

* Local Government Finance vol 76 no 4 April 1972

specific projects required by the Chief Executive or the management team.

O & M

7.8   There is no similar argument, in our view, for placing O and M staff under the day to day control of line managers, not least because the subject covers a wider field than that of a work study team. It seems to us that the basic nature of the function too is different. O and M is concerned with the structure of an organisational unit and the way in which that unit operates to achieve its objectives; an O and M function within that organisational unit is less likely to be able to exercise independent judgment than an 'outside' team. The latter will also benefit from the wider range of assignments open to a central team.

7.9   Organisationally we recommend that the O and M unit should be under the wing of the head of administration, but it should be very much an aid to the Chief Executive and the management team. It should, we believe, operate to a programme laid down by the management team, though that programme will need to be sufficiently flexible to enable urgent ad hoc assignments to be undertaken. In particular the unit would have an important role to play in keeping organisational structures, not only of departments, but of the authority itself, up to date and in line with changing requirements. Reports of O and M teams upon any individual department should initially be submitted to the head of that department. If it is necessary for a report to go beyond him it should be submitted direct to the Chief Executive for consideration by the management team. It should not in the first instance go to the head of administration since this would purport to place him in a position superior to that of the head of department under review.

Computers

7.10 Although the computer in one sense can be included in the generic title of management services, because of its close link with financial and payroll questions it is normally found within the Treasurer's department. Generally speaking we see no reason to change this, but we do see substantial disadvantages in allowing its use to be dictated by the head of the department in which it happens to be situated. We therefore suggest that the use of computer time and facilities should be controlled by a separate body responsible direct to the management team.

Research and Intelligence

7.11 The Local Government Bill gives to the county councils a wide permissive power to carry out research and collect information on any matters concerning the county. The powers of district councils in this respect are slightly more limited in that they may only incur expenditure on research and the collection of information in connection with the exercise of their statutory functions.

7.12 At county level a strategic information and research function may well develop which might require the creation of a central Research and Intelligence Unit staffed by suitably qualified officers. Such units already exist in some authorities. We are aware of the approach taken by one large authority. It has recently extended the research function to each of its major departments who now have a research section for their own service requirements. In addition, however, a small Research and Intelligence Unit is located in the Clerk's Department. Its work programme ensures that it carries out only research not undertaken in any other department, for example, on local government reorganisation and identifying statistics used throughout the authority. The purpose of the Unit is four-fold:

i.   To provide effective information for managers: for example to present management statistics in terms meaningful to the layman; to indicate economic and social trends in the county compared with those at national level.

ii. Miscellaneous intelligence: for example, to identify key future events in the authority's area and to relate their impact; to keep abreast of new management and research development elsewhere.

iii. To provide a consultancy service to departments: for example, upon methods of research and specialist systems of forecasting—eg future primary school population; undertaking ad hoc projects as frequently requested both by county departments and district council authorities.

iv. Corporate Planning: for example, assisting in setting departmental objectives, identifying community needs, and devising measures of output and performance.

7.13 Most district councils will depend partly on the data assembled by properly trained staff whom we suggest should be placed within the various programme areas, and partly on that assembled by any county unit. There is clearly some danger of duplication of research effort, and to avoid this we suggest that each authority should maintain a central record of information and research findings to which reference could be made before new work is undertaken. Such a record would include not only data assembled by that authority's own departments, but also notes of, for example, research findings of other authorities and central agencies.

Organisation of management services

7.14 Because so much of the evidence submitted is based on the premise that management services cover only O and M and work study we have found it difficult to derive from it any conclusions about the way in which the wider concept of management services should be reflected in the organisation structure. Such evidence as we have received on this subject suggests that the pendulum may be swinging away from the idea that all management services should be centralised into one monolithic department. Some papers have suggested that there should be wider use of management services within individual departments and we have received criticism of the growth of central management services departments on the grounds that they have become a very costly item and that the expected benefits have not been realised. It is said that their cost benefits have not been established.

7.15 Mr. J. D. Hender, Chief Executive of Coventry CBC, suggested to us that the concept of a central management services unit was a necessary step in management development in local government but that it

"is now rather old-fashioned and has no real place in a corporate management organisation".

He went on to say that:

"Corporate management implies that the responsibility for effective management rests in departments, who then contribute to the corporate system, and it is in the departments that the techniques must be developed and used. (These techniques) should be regarded as part of the tools of normal working and not as specialised instruments called in from a central unit for a particular purpose."

7.16 Others have drawn exactly the opposite conclusion on the consequences of the implementation of corporate management, maintaining that the need for a corporate approach makes it all the more necessary that there should be one centralised service. The Local Government Personnel and Management Services Group, for example, commenting on the use and limitations of management services said:

"The initial limitation, we would suggest, is in fact the fragmentation of the various services which occurs in many authorities."

7.17 We have received evidence from several sources which amounts almost to a compromise between these two views. According to this view, the various techniques fall naturally into a number of groups each of which performs a different function. The London Borough of Greenwich, for example, has grouped Work Study, O and M, Operational Research and Job Evaluation with the Establishment Group of services; PPBS, Cost Benefit Analysis, Consumer Research and PERT networks with the section responsible for advising the Chief Executive on forward planning and the various financially based "cost-benefit" techniques are under the control of the Director of Finance and Borough Treasurer.

7.18 In another authority it is suggested that there are similarly three elements to Management Services:

a)   Establishment control services

b)   Services which support the management process

c)   Techniques to analyse or solve individual problems.

7.19 The London Boroughs' Management Services Unit, who commented that in existing Management Services Departments, O and M, Work Study and Systems Analysis "even when under the direction of a single officer usually operate separately", have also distinguished between management appraisal and financial appraisal techniques, though it must also be said that the Unit envisages that in the long term the two might be brought together into an integrated group.

7.20 Faced with these various alternatives, each of which is said to be well suited to the needs of the various authorities making use of it, we find it impossible to be dogmatic, but we find ourselves inclined more to Mr. Hender's view than to that which favours the bringing together of all management services in one unit. It seems to us that services to management may validly reside in various places; for example one might place the computer and the finance based techniques with the Treasurer's department, O and M together with the central work study unit and any central research and intelligence unit under the head of administration, and other techniques similarly within appropriate departments.

7.21 Wherever the relevant specialists are located, we see increasing scope for teams from the various departments contributing to the examination and appraisal of programmes or projects under consideration by the management team. We were told that Grimsby CBC have made it a matter of policy that

"all Chief Officers place their specialist staff at the disposal of the Town Clerk and Chief Executive and the Chief Officers' Group and we try to maintain a degree of flexibility and fluidity in the deployment of specialist staff in this way."

7.22 This illustrates the dual role of management services staff. On the one hand their skills may be deployed within the departments where they are most required, but they must also, of necessity be available to central management. In this latter role they will operate according to the programmes and requirements of the management team, notwithstanding that for administrative purposes they are employed within particular departments.

Monitoring of performance

7.23 We have referred several times in this report to the need to monitor performance against planned programmes and this principle applies equally to the field of management services. In order to ensure that the authority derives the maximum benefit from these services, par-ticularly those of the computer, there must be a realistic and continuous appraisal of the way in which they are used and the results which they produce. It is all too easy to perpetuate processes which have long outlived their original purpose, or to collect and assemble data for which there is no longer any real use. Management services must be as ready to justify its own expenditure as it is to require others to do so.

Corporate Planning Unit

7.24 We have heard from a number of sources that in the past local authorities have given too much attention to operating the services for which they are responsible and too little to planning them. It is of the essence of the corporate approach to management which we are advocating that there should be a realistic attempt to plan ahead on an authority-wide basis, to formulate objectives, evaluate alternative methods of achieving those objectives and measure the effectiveness of ultimate performance against those objectives.

7.25 We have already referred in paragraph 5.44 to a Corporate Planning Group which operates through various sub-groups and is responsible to the Chief Officers Group. It is appropriate here to set out in more detail some of the Group's terms of reference:

    i.   Identification, formulation and review of objectives;

    ii.   evaluation of short term programmes aimed at achieving those objectives;

    iii.   consideration of priorities within those programmes as between different services;

iv.   formulation of proposals for linking presentation of objectives, programmes and budgets;

v.   developing longer term plans;

vi.   monitoring and reviewing progress as against plans.

7.26 Stockport CBC have adopted a different approach by the appointment of a Corporate Planning Co-ordinator who

"will be concerned mainly with bringing together the plans developed by the various divisions, but will also conduct special studies where required, monitor achievements against plans and help to determine the appropriate long range objectives and near-term targets at which (the authority) should be aiming."

The Corporate Planning Co-ordinator is on the staff of the Director of Administration and has no junior corporate planning staff.

7.27 Liverpool CBC have appointed a Director of Programme Planning whose responsibilities appear to be broadly similar to those of the Stockport officer, but who operates through a number of Programme Planning Assistants.

7.28 Both the Stockport and Liverpool appointments are relatively recent and we do not feel that their full effect can yet be evaluated, but generally we believe that there is much to be gained by involving officers from the various departments of the authority directly in the corporate planning process, rather than creating a separate permanent unit staffed by 'professional' corporate planners. By this means the corporate planning unit will be kept in close touch with the reality of what is actually happening on the ground and those officers from within departments who serve within the unit will be given valuable experience in the broad management problems of the authority as a whole.

7.29 The terms of reference of the unit might well be something on the lines of those set out in paragraph 7.25, covering both the planning and monitoring aspects of corporate management.

7.30 The work of the Corporate Planning Unit will take up a substantial part of the time of its members. This means additional costs, both in terms of money and staff and authorities must recognise this

In the long run, however, any additional cost should be more than compensated by improvements in efficiency and effectiveness of performance.

7.31 In some Districts, of course, this degree of sophistication will not be justified, but the need to plan ahead, set objectives and measure performance is nonetheless important. It will be the responsibility of the Chief Executive and the management team to see that the necessary machinery is set up to facilitate this.

Central administration and secretariat

7.32 The responsibility for the central administrative department has hitherto been that of the Clerk, but in view of our strong recommendation that the Chief Executive should be divorced from departmental responsibility it is necessary to create a separate department to carry out the function. In a number of authorities the head of administration, as we have somewhat anonymously referred to him in earlier parts of this report, has been designated Director of Administration. That title seems reasonable in a management structure where the term 'director' is used to designate the principal chief officers, but does not, in our view, really cover the role which this officer plays.

7.33 The prime roles of the department are to provide a secretariat for the Council, for all committees and for the management team and to assist the Chief Executive in his co-ordinative capacity. Furthermore there are certain specialist services used in the management process, for example, Research and Intelligence, Organisation and Methods, Work Study, Project Control, which do not justify the rating of separate departmental status. In the interests of administrative efficiency these services should, in our view, be located as sections within the department for day-to-day control and to provide the necessary internal supervision. Notwithstanding this organisational arrangement, however, these services should be deployed by and be accountable to the management team. In addition the department will carry administrative responsibility for certain other services which need to be centrally administered but which do not, themselves, justify a separate department. Local circumstances will largely dictate what these services are, but legal services, public relations, registration functions and archives services might well be examples. This department could also be responsible for providing common office services for all departments.

7.34 We suggest that the head of the central administrative department is rather analogous to the secretary of a company and the title of County (or District) Secretary seems to us to be an apt one. In our structural diagrams in Chapter 9 we have therefore used this title in all diagrams except those where the title 'director' is used to designate the principal chief officers. In those cases we have retained the title 'Director of Administration'.

Public Relations and Information Services

7.35 We believe that the forthcoming reorganisation of local government will bring into sharp focus the deficiencies of public relations within many local authorities. In our view the public have a right to information about the affairs of their local council and access to committee and council meetings may well stimulate the public's desire to be better informed.

7.36 A number of local authorities have, of course, given specific recognition to the importance of public relations by the appointment of Public Relations Officers, the setting up of information centres, the publication of news sheets and other means, but our impression is that a great many authorities have paid insufficient regard to this function. This may be due to the doubt which exists in some areas about the propriety of some PR methods used in other spheres. We are in no doubt however that local authorities have a firm duty to inform the community of their activities and to put the Council's view on matters of concern to that community.

7.37 The Institute of Public Relations Local Government Group in their evidence to us included a list of functions performed by Public Relations Units in local government. In a situation where, we are told, only 100 local authorities have established full-time public relations sections, we believe that it would be useful for this list to be given wider circulation and we accordingly reproduce it at Appendix K. We do not necessarily endorse the inclusion of every item on the Group's list.

7.38 We suggest that all the larger local authorities should set up a full-time public relations and information unit, headed by a suitably qualified officer. We recognise that in some of the smaller authorities such a unit may consist only of one man and in the smallest even that might not be justified, but it is nonetheless important that the duty to provide information should not only be recognised but should be demonstrated. In those smallest authorities it should be one of the responsibilities of the Chief Executive to see that proper channels of communication are established in both directions and that both public and press have access to an officer of sufficient knowledge and authority to deal with their enquiries.

7.39 Above all we suggest that local authorities should themselves adopt, as far as possible, an outgoing and positive attitude to the members of the community which they serve and should provide adequate resources, both finance and staff, to facilitate this. It has been suggested to us that authorities should publish an annual report to their electorate each year. Such a report might contain not only factual information in relation to the utilisation of the resources of the authority but also a narrative section in which the authority would identify the major problems facing it and the plans it had for solving them. A report of this nature would enable the local electorate to judge the performance of the authority in relation to its declared plans and programmes.

7.40 We have received evidence about the status of the head of the Public Relations Unit, both from the Institute of Public Relations and from other sources. Opinions vary about this and local circumstances will play a large part in determining the PRO's status. One can envisage, for example, that the post of PRO in a tourist area would be a particularly important one. We do not propose to make any specific recommendation on this subject, though clearly the PRO must be of adequate standing to carry out his job. Mr. R. S. Parsons, PRO of Northumberland County Council summed it up in his evidence to us as follows:

"The Public Relations Adviser should have ready access to the Chairman of the Council, Party leaders, committee chairmen and top managers, and be of sufficient calibre, both personally and in public relations experience, to command their respect".

Dissemination of information internally

7.41 It is not only in the dissemination of information to the public and Press that local authorities have a responsibility. They also have a responsibility to keep their own staff informed, particularly on matters which have, or are believed to have, a direct bearing upon them. This is important at a time of organisational change within the authority and particularly at a time of simultaneous organisational change within every authority such as is now facing local government staff.

7.42 We have been dismayed to see and hear how little staff have been told in the past about some proposed local reorganisations, as well as how little many authorities are doing to keep staff informed about progress on the present one. Some authorities have published news sheets, some have regular meetings either with the staff (in the smaller authorities) or with their representatives, but many appear to have done little or nothing. This is not just a question of the interests of the staff, important though these are. The success or failure of any organisational change depends largely on the willingness of the staff to make it work. If management neglects its responsibility to keep staff informed it can hardly be surprised if they put their own interpretation on such information, probably inaccurate, as reaches them through unofficial channels. We were told by an officer in one authority which had undergone a reorganisation that staff

"became apprehensive about their own positions. Ill-informed, insecure and confused they became antagonistic to the whole reorganisation".

The responsibility for such an unhappy situation rests squarely with management, and the remedy is in its own hands. There must be the fullest possible information to members of the staff; how this is done is relatively unimportant provided that it is done.

7.43 We have deliberately laid great emphasis on the particular circumstances of reorganisation, but much can and should be done to keep staff informed of what is happening within the authority in more normal times. Some authorities already do this through regular meetings between staff and senior officers or by circulation of brief synopses of news concerning the authority, and we commend such practices to all authorities.

7.44 We have referred earlier in this report to the importance of an adequate flow of information to the elected members. The need for this has become more and more apparent as our enquiries have progressed and we make no apology for referring to it again.

7.45 We have received evidence of a number of means by which elected members are either supplied with, or can obtain, information about specific matters. One authority publishes a brief synopsis of items of current interest covering not only internal affairs of the County Council, but also items appearing in the local and national Press and central Government decisions considered to be of particular interest. More detailed information is available on request in respect of any listed items. In another case each member has a supply of prepaid enquiry forms which enable him to raise enquiries on any facet of the Council's activities. Many authorities have set up members' information rooms in which detailed information about all matters concerning the work of the authority is available. All this, of course, is in addition to the normal circulation of appropriate committee reports and minutes.

7.46 It may well be a function of a Public Relations Unit to organise the provision of information to members, but if that is not the case we recommend that it should be a specific responsibility of one officer of suitable calibre.

Supplies

7.47 We do not propose to rehearse again the arguments in favour of one department charged with the central purchasing of supplies and equipment; these are, we feel, well enough known already. At District level particularly, however, we would urge consideration of the benefits to be gained by use of the purchasing facilities of the County Council or, failing this, by forming consortia. Authorities which themselves run large central purchasing departments should ensure that the activities of such departments are subject to the same scrutiny as regards both expenditure and cost effectiveness as other departments.

Land and Buildings

7.48 Land and buildings are among the most expensive and scarce resources of a local authority and the efficient management of these resources is a matter of first importance. In many authorities the management of existing land and buildings will be a substantial task, which, coupled with the acquisition and disposal programme, may well justify the existence of a separate major department closely linked to the land utilisation sub-committee of the policy and resources committee. We have in mind particularly authorities with a substantial investment in land and buildings and also authorities with large town/city centre redevelopment programmes in hand.

7.49 Each authority should create and maintain a central record of all estate owned, and should co-ordinate all forward land acquisition and disposal proposals in order to maximise the use of existing estate. In particular consideration should be given, wherever possible, to the combination of separate acquisition and building proposals on to one site, in order to achieve savings in building costs and in common services and for the convenience of the public.

7.50 Through their land utilisation sub-committees authorities should also consider carefully and keep under review the economic use of existing property. Changing local circumstances may suggest that it would be more economic to sell or redevelop existing sites and re-build on a different site where the demand can equally well be met. The possibility of combining commercial and public uses should not be overlooked.

Secretarial Services to Members

7.51 At an earlier point in this report we emphasised the importance of the role of the member in representing his electoral area. Such duties can take up a substantial amount of members' own time, not only in following up requests for information or complaints about this or that aspect of the Council's activities, but also in stimulating interest in the affairs of the authority through ward meetings, surgeries etc. In this role the member is acting as much in the interests of the

90

authority as of his constituents and we can see no good reason why the authority should not assist him with the correspondence in which his duties involve him.

7.52 Some authorities already provide some facilities for members, but in very few is there anything approaching a comprehensive service. We recommend that in all authorities provision should be made for basic secretarial services to be available to members.

General

7.53 We have in this chapter dealt only with those central services for which we recommend a change of structure or management. We have not made reference to other central services, particularly finance, for which we do not contemplate any major structural change.

Chapter 8

Working arrangements between the new authorities—The 'Community' Approach

8.1 In the course of our enquiries we have seen and heard a great deal about the conflict and general lack of co-operation which is said to exist between authorities in some areas at the present time and there has been, in the evidence submitted to us, a recognition that authorities must in the future establish much closer working relationships than in the past.

8.2 The Local Government Bill itself provides a broad and flexible framework for the establishment of local co-operation through, for example, its provisions dealing with the discharge of functions and the placing of staff at the disposal of other authorities. A great deal has been said and written about the extent to which the new authorities will make use of the provisions relating to the discharge of functions. It is beyond our terms of reference to suggest how local authorities might arrange for the discharge of particular functions, since this is essentially a matter for local decision. What we wish to consider is the relationship which should exist between the various authorities and the organisational machinery necessary to promote and maintain that relationship.

8.3 We have, throughout this report, urged local authorities to adopt a corporate approach to the management of their affairs. We believe that there is in many ways an equal need for what has been termed a 'community' approach to the problems and needs of areas. We are not, however, suggesting that there should be an attempt to organise all services or plan all projects according to some detailed formal plan; the need as we see it is for each authority to be aware of and take into account the interaction between the plans, policies and functions for which it is responsible and those of other authorities. In a recent discussion paper on the organisation of the new county councils, * Basildon UDC stated:

* _The new Counties—The Same or Different?"—Basildon UDC, May 1972._

"... if the community is to benefit from local government reorganisation, then the closest co-operation must be maintained at all levels within the county organisation and between county and district councils. It is vital that at the 'grass roots' there should be a complete understanding of the reasons for policy decisions and also a means of testing reaction to those decisions and constantly assessing needs".

8.4 We believe that this concept of 'community' interest must involve not only the new local authorities, but also other voluntary and public agencies, including particularly the new area health boards and regional water authorities. Our main task, however, is to relate the concept to management within local government, and we suggest that it is from local government that the initial effort must come.

8.5 At member level the need for a community approach seems to us to arise in two ways, first in the interaction and interrelationship of functions allocated to the counties and districts respectively, and second in relation to their overall policies and plans.

8.6 We recommend that there should be a district joint committee of county and district members for each district within the county to co-ordinate the interaction of all county and district functions and policies for the locality. Two examples of matters which could come before this committee are the co-ordination of the county social services and the district housing functions and the respective functions of each authority in relation to planning. Other areas of activity or of need will appear where both authorities have a role to play and where those roles must be complementary. Arrangements for the discharge of functions will clearly be a matter for consideration by such a committee.

8.7 As an alternative we considered whether there should be district joint committees in respect of each major function or service but we concluded that such committees might lead to the development of a narrow functional attitude inconsistent with the broad corporate and community approaches to which we attach such importance.

8.8 For similar reasons we do not believe that the county representatives on the district joint committees which we have proposed in paragraph 8.6 should only be those from within the relevant district. Certainly the county contingent should include members with knowledge of and interest in the district, but there should also be some 'uncommitted' members in order to ensure that the wider viewpoint is not lost sight of.

8.9   We see these committees as essentially deliberative and advisory bodies whose function is to facilitate joint discussion, joint action and the exchange of information between the two spheres of local government. They would have a particularly important role to play in respect of concurrent functions. In order to promote the idea of partnership and equality in the meetings we suggest that the joint committees should be serviced by the district council staff and that the Chief Executive of the district should make the appropriate arrangements.

8.10 In addition to these district joint committees we also see a need for co-ordination and joint planning of the broad overall policies of the county and the districts within it. Professor John Stewart, of the Institute of Local Government Studies, said in a recent article* :—

"Objectives should not be set by one authority in isolation. .... What is sought is joint planning, not just a joint plan. It must be recognised that there will be different authorities with different objectives who will not always agree. The outcome of joint planning may be greater awareness and understanding rather than agreement. But that will be a step forward."

8.11 The district joint committees which we have been discussing will provide a partial base upon which to build this joint planning structure, but we believe that there should also be in each county a permanent joint committee comprising leading members of the policy and resources committees of the county and of each district. This county joint committee might well only meet two or three times in each year, but we recommend that it should meet on a regular rather than an ad hoc basis. It will thus provide a continuing forum for joint policy discussions and avoid the implication that it only meets to sort out disputes and difficulties between the county and the districts.

8.12 The general principles of the preceding paragraphs apply with equal force to metropolitan and non-metropolitan counties. It may however be that in the metropolitan counties the more concentrated nature of the county area and the consequent greater community of interest will mean that the county joint committee referred to in the preceding paragraph will carry out also the functions which we have outlined in paragraph 8.6.

* *"New separation or new co-operation?"*—*Local Government Chronicle vol 117 no. 5481 17/3/72*

8.13 However authorities choose to adapt the basic formula to their own particular situation, the important thing is that some formal machinery should be set up to ensure that each new authority does not concentrate solely on its own needs and problems to the exclusion of those of the wider community.

8.14 So far we have concentrated exclusively on the role of the member in promoting and achieving an inter-authority organisation to assist in community planning. At officer level there are already meetings of groups which cross authority boundaries, but these tend to be oriented on a professional rather than inter-authority basis. Such meetings perform a very useful role in widening professional knowledge and experience and may, even if only incidentally promote the sort of relationship which we wish to see established. We would like, however, to see more formal and regular meetings between officers at county and district level to parallel the joint committees of members. In some instances such meetings will continue to be on a professional basis, but we would also recommend regular meetings between the Chief Executives of the county and its constituent districts and even joint meetings of the management teams of the county and either individual districts or small groups of districts. Such meetings would, amongst other things, serve to explore matters for discussion by the joint committees referred to in paragraph 8.6.

8.15 Authorities in each sphere should also make the fullest use of the particular expertise of the other. To quote again briefly from Professor Stewart's article* :

"Consideration of alternatives to meet ... objectives should not be restricted to the activities and resources of a single authority. Each will have specialist skills, information and resources which others will lack".

8.16 In the field of public transport, for example, the non-metropolitan counties have a new responsibility to co-ordinate the provision of public transport within their areas. The need for this to be taken into account in their general transportation planning will mean that they will require expertise which will probably not be readily available within the county council structure. It may well prove difficult to recruit properly qualified senior staff for the county, but the necessary expertise is, however, likely to be on hand in the management of municipal public transport undertakings within the county districts, and also in nationalised and private undertakings. There would seem to

* op. cit. in paragraph 8.10

us to be merit in making use of that expertise, even if only on a part-time advisory basis, rather than attempting to recruit scarce full-time officers.

8.17 Across the whole field of what might be termed 'central services' eg computers, supplies, valuation etc there is scope for provision of services by one authority for another, and we have already referred to the possibility of area offices of the county councils being provided with common services by district council staff. The arrangements may flow in either direction and the extent to which such arrangements are to be made will require early consideration in the run up to re-organisation and early decision by the new authorities. It is essential that the county and district Joint Reorganisation Committees to be set up under the Local Government Bill should reach an understanding on these matters as soon as possible. Our comments at paragraph 6.26 regarding secondments of staff between authorities are also in point.

8.18 We have already said that we do not intend to suggest how the agency provisions might be used by the new authorities, but this again will be an area where an early decision will be required because of the wider implications which will flow from it. More generally on agency, we understand that arrangements made will be terminable, and any arrangement which proves to be ineffective will obviously require to be terminated. There will, however, be substantial implications for skilled staff in any such termination and on management grounds we therefore urge authorities to ensure that whatever agency arrangements they make are not lightly reversed and are kept under review by the district joint committees which we recommended in paragraph 8.6.

8.19 Earlier in this chapter we mentioned briefly the fundamental need for co-operation and co-ordination of policies and functions with the area health authorities and regional water authorities. Because of the contiguity of the boundaries of the former with those of local govern-ment it will be a simple matter structurally to involve the area health authorities in those services of mutual concern both in the day to day operation and in the forward planning and policy making of local au-thorities, particularly through the district joint committees to which we have referred earlier. At officer level too, the community physician must be kept abreast of much, if not all, of all local authority proposals and his advice will frequently be needed by the authority's management team, particularly on matters in the field of environmental health.

8.20 At the time of drafting this report consultations were still in progress about formal collaboration arrangements between area health authorities and their corresponding local authorities and decisions had not been announced on the arrangements for the school health services. It follows that our somewhat general suggestions in this field will need to be reviewed and expanded in the light of developments and in particular of the legislation giving effect to the NHS reorganisation.

8.21 Unlike the proposed area health authorities, the boundaries of regional water authorities are not contiguous with local government boundaries. It would nonetheless be quite possible for the county joint committees to include representatives of the appropriate water authority(ies). There might also be a need for some separate co-ordinative body comprising the regional water authority and representatives of all local authorities within its area. As with the county joint committees, any such body should, we suggest, meet according to a regular timetable and not just when particular problems arise. The appropriate officer of the regional water authority will be in a similar position vis à vis the management team as that which we have suggested for the community physician in relation to health matters.

Chapter 9

The new authorities—Functions and possible management structures ·

Introduction

9.1   The major functions allocated to the various authorities at the time of drafting this report are those shown at Appendix L. If the allocation of any of those functions is amended in the later stages of the Local Government Bill's progress through Parliament, some of the detail in this chapter will require amendment.

9.2   It is not our intention to lay down one structure which all authorities should adopt, but everything that has gone before in this report leads inevitably to certain basic structural features which we recommend should be common to all authorities.

9.3   The first of these is the Policy and Resources Committee, supported by its four sub-committees, viz:

Finance   responsible for day to day finance matters.

Personnel   responsible for establishment and personnel activities.

Land   responsible for questions of land/building acquisition, utilisation and disposal.

Performance   responsible for the monitoring of results against
Review   objectives and appraisal of standards, calling
                   committees and officers to account (see para. 4.20).

Major issues from any of the sub-committees would be referred to the parent policy and resources committee. Each of these sub-committees should comprise members of the policy and resources and members of other committees. In our view, for the reasons given in paragraph 4.18 there should be a substantial representation of members of the Council who do not serve on the policy and resources committee.

9.4   The other important common feature at member level does not appear in the structure diagrams which follow. We have referred on a number of occasions to informal groups of members being set up for particular purposes both within and between programme areas. By their very nature these groups are not part of the formal structure of the authority, but the structures which we suggest will provide ample opportunity for such groups to be created.

9.5   At officer level too there are similar common features. The Chief Executive, supported by his management team, is basic to our conception of the management process in the new authorities and appears, therefore, in each of our diagrams.

9.6   The framework within which we have designed our structures is depicted in outline in the following diagrams.

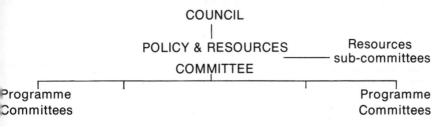

Diagram 1 (a) Outline Committee Structure

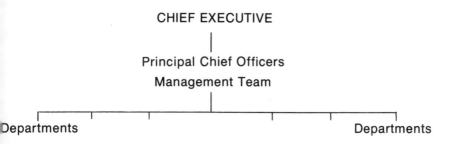

Diagram 1 (b) - Outline Departmental Structure

9.7   Within these frameworks wide variations in structure are possible. In illustrating possible adaptations, we have not attempted to include every function of every authority, but have confined ourselves to what seem to us to be major functions. The allocation of those functions between committees too is capable of variations to suit local circumstances and our allocation should not be treated as definitive. In our committee structure for a county, for example, we have placed the library, museums and art galleries functions with the Education Committee and refuse disposal, gipsy sites and caravan sites with the Amenities and Countryside Committee. It could be argued that the former should be under the Amenities and Countryside Committee and the latter under Planning and Transportation.

9.8 In our departmental structures we have similarly shown only the major departments. The various minor departments will generally be placed under the general administrative umbrella of one or other major department. In our county structure, for example, the Archivist might, particularly if he is responsible for current records, be placed under the County Secretary. The titles which we use in our diagrams throughout are illustrative of the function only and are not definitive of title. The latter will be a matter for local choice.

The non-metropolitan county

9.9 The first type of authority which we consider is the non-metropolitan county, and one possible committee structure is illustrated in diagram 2 (a).

9.10 In this structure the allocation of major functions between the various programme committees is as follows:

Education	Education
	Libraries
	Museums
	Art Galleries
Social Services	Social Services
Planning and	Planning
Transportation	Highways & Transport Planning
	Traffic
	Parking
	Road Safety

100

For a full description of the relationship between the Council, the policy and resources committee and the programme committees reference must be made to the main text, particularly paragraphs 4.1, 4.4, 4.14, 4.15, 4.18, 4.22 and Appendix H.

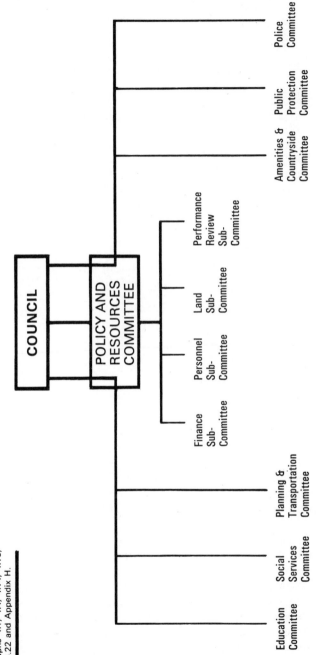

Diagram 2(a) — Committee structure — Non-metropolitan county

Notes: 1. A separate National Parks committee will be required in appropriate counties.
2. The Police committee is the police authority, but by convention it is expected that it will use the same lines of communication as other committees. The diagram reflects this.

	Lighting
	Aerodromes
	Public Transport Co-ordination
Amenities and Countryside	Country Parks
	Footpaths & Bridleways (not road footways)
	Commons
	Caravan Sites
	Gipsy Sites
	Recreation and Tourism
	Smallholdings
	Land Drainage
	Refuse Disposal
	Entertainment
Public Protection	Consumer Protection
	Emergency Services
	Health Education
	Registration and Licensing
National Parks (if appropriate)	National Parks
Police	Police

9.11 We are aware that there will in many cases be substantial pressure for a separate Highways Committee but we believe that the essential co-ordination between the various aspects of strategic planning and transportation is more likely to be achieved under one committee.

9.12 In this structure we have grouped many of the 'leisure' functions within the Amenities and Countryside Committee but with the increasing emphasis on this subject local authorities may well decide that a separate committee for leisure is required. The functions of such a committee would require careful definition because of the wide range of activities which could be included within the 'leisure' area. We see particular demarcation problems because of the close link with the education programme area in respect of, for example, the use of school recreational facilities and the increasing popularity of evening classes as a joint educational and leisure activity.

9.13 One possible departmental structure associated with the committee structure in diagram 2(a) is shown in diagram 2(b).

9.14 In this structure, there are no 'directors' and the Principal Chief Officers do not have authority over other Chief Officers. The latter would have direct access to the appropriate committee(s) but on major matters would go through the management team. They would be called in to assist the management team on matters within their sphere of responsibility. The diagram in fact represents no more than an array of possible departments with an indication of which Chief Officers are likely to be members of the management team. It is not intended to carry any implications about the relative positions of the various Chief Officers shown, each of whom is directly responsible to the Chief Executive.

9.15 It is possible that in some authorities there will be a separate appointment of County Solicitor, and in that event he would, we suggest, also rank as a Chief Officer. In other authorities, particularly those in which the County Secretary is a lawyer, the position will be as we suggest in paragraph 7.33 and the legal services will be provided by a section of the Secretary's department.

9.16 In diagram 2(c) we illustrate an alternative departmental structure in which some departments are grouped together under directors. We have not found it possible to group all departments in this way and following our reasoning in paragraph 5.73 some therefore remain independent. Their position vis à vis both committees and the management team is exactly the same as that of the Non-Principal Chief Officers referred to in paragraph 9.14.

9.17 This structure represents a system of management about which we have received evidence from some authorities. We recognise that, notwithstanding the common title of 'Director' the directors are not in fact occupying positions with precisely similar roles. The Director of Social Services is, of course, a statutory officer heading one department, though it could be argued that his present department, prior to 1970, comprised several independent departments. The Director of Technical Services heads a group of four formerly separate departments and has line responsibility for them. If it is felt that this would create too large a directorate it would be possible to divide it into two separate directorates, one covering planning and transportation, the other land and architectural services. The Director of Finance is indistinguishable

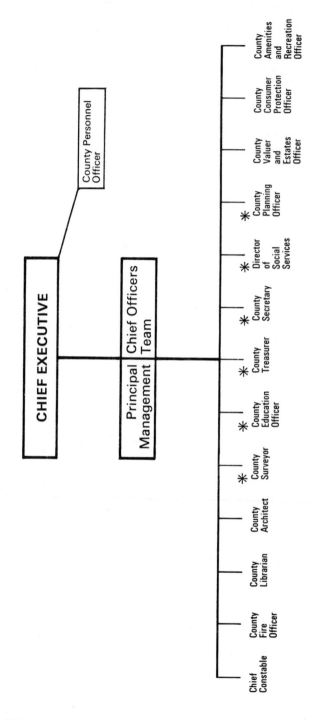

Diagram 2(b) — Departmental structure A — Non-metropolitan county

CHIEF EXECUTIVE

County Personnel Officer

Principal Chief Officers Management Team

Chief Constable

County Fire Officer

County Librarian

County Architect

County Surveyor *

County Education Officer *

County Treasurer *

County Secretary *

Director of Social Services *

County Planning Officer *

County Valuer and Estates Officer

County Consumer Protection Officer

County Amenities and Recreation Officer

* Members of management team

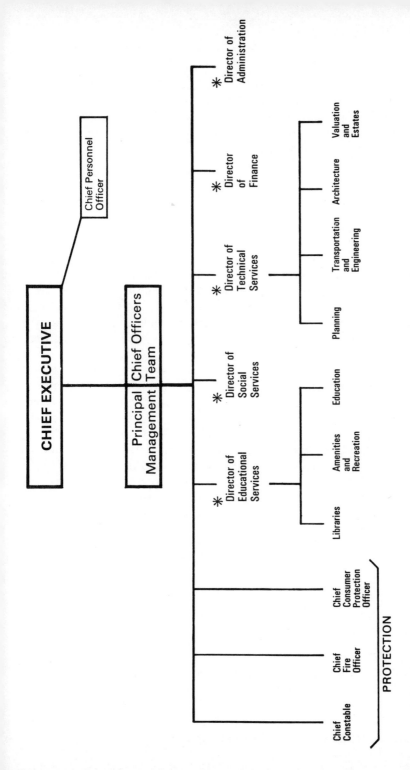

Diagram 2(c) — Departmental structure B — Non-metropolitan county

from the County Treasurer in Diagram 2(b), and the Director of Administration is identical with the County Secretary in that diagram. It is because of the problems which seem to us to be inherent in this type of structure that we have the reservations about it which we expressed in paragraph 5.73.

The Metropolitan County

9.18 The role of the metropolitan county is likely to be in many ways different from that of its non-metropolitan counterpart. On the one hand it has fewer statutory functions in its own right, and on the other it has a far more compact area with problems and needs which, generally speaking, are far more likely to be common right across the county.

9.19 The first of these factors means that the committee structure required for the exercise of the council's statutory functions is extremely simple, as Diagram 3(a) indicates.

9.20 The four resource utilisation sub-committees of the Policy and Resources Committee carry out the same functions as those of the non-metropolitan county and those of the Police Committee are self evident. The other two committees have the following major functions:

Planning and Transportation	Planning Highways and Transport Planning Traffic Parking Road Safety Street Lighting Refuse Disposal Aerodromes
Public Protection	Consumer Protection Emergency Services Health Education

9.21 Our comments about the Planning and Transportation Committee

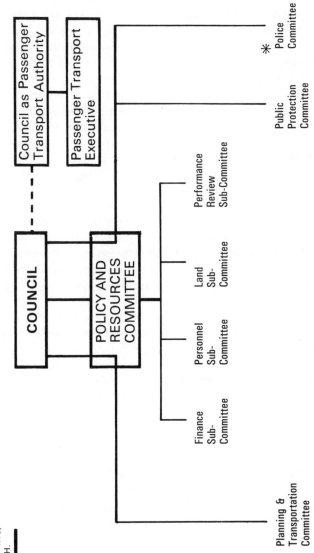

IMPORTANT
This diagram is illustrative only. For a full description of the relationship between the Council, the policy and resources committee and the programme committees reference must be made to the main text, particularly paragraphs 4.1, 4.4, 4.14, 4.15, 4.18, 4.22 and Appendix H.

COUNCIL

Council as Passenger Transport Authority

Passenger Transport Executive

POLICY AND RESOURCES COMMITTEE

Finance Sub-Committee

Personnel Sub-Committee

Land Sub-Committee

Performance Review Sub-Committee

Planning & Transportation Committee

Public Protection Committee

Police Committee

✻

✻ See Note 2 to Diagram 2(a)

Diagram 3(a) – Committee structure – Metropolitan county

in the non-metropolitan county (see paragraph 9.11) apply equally to the metropolitan county. The Council is, of course, also the Passenger Transport Authority and we have therefore illustrated this role in our diagram.

9.22 In this structure we have excluded many of the functions exercisable concurrently with the metropolitan districts, particularly those falling within the broad amenity/recreation heading. We suggest that in metropolitan areas particularly such functions will be more appropriate to the district level, but this is a matter which the joint committees which we recommended in Chapter 8 should establish at an early date.

9.23 At first sight, therefore, the metropolitan county would appear to have a limited range of tasks, particularly at member level, though of course the two committees referred to in the preceding paragraphs cover very important functions. We suggest, however, that for the reasons given in paragraph 9.18 the metropolitan county is particularly well placed to promote and co-ordinate a total approach to the substantial urban problems of its area and that the county should as and when required set up groups of members to examine and report back on particular needs and problems. In the first place such groups would report back to the Policy and Resources Committee of the county, but their findings would clearly be fruitful subjects for discussion at the joint county/district policy committee.

9.24 A possible departmental structure would be that shown in Diagram 3(b).

9.25 We do not show any alternative structure for the metropolitan county because the range of statutory functions does not in our view justify any grouping of departments under directors. We envisage, therefore, that the basic structure will be on the lines which we have illustrated.

9.26 In a metropolitan county we would generally expect that the legal function would be incorporated within the department of the County Secretary and that a separate legal department would not be required. We have not shown the Director of the Passenger Transport Executive in our diagram, since the PTE is not a department of the council. The Director will, however, work closely with the officers of the council in many aspects of their work and will, no doubt, join the discussions

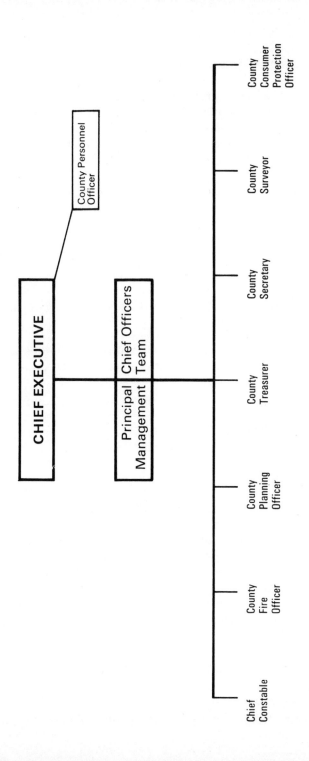

Diagram 3(b) — Departmental structure — Metropolitan county

Note : Logically the members of the management team\would be the Planning Officer, Treasurer, Secretary and Surveyor, but in view of the limited range of departments authorities may wish to include all the chief officers.

of the management team on appropriate occasions.

9.27 The Chief Executive of a strategic planning authority like the metropolitan county is perhaps more likely to have an engineering or planning background than in other authorities, but even if he is professionally qualified in one of these fields he should not have particular responsibility for those areas of the authority's affairs.

9.28 We have not included an architect or an estates officer within our suggested structure, but in some counties such appointments may be desirable. We envisage, however, that in many instances the districts will provide the requisite services for the county, or that they will be obtained from private sources.

The Metropolitan District

9.29 In the metropolitan district, analysis of the statutory functions suggests that there would be six major areas of activity, viz:

> Development
> Housing
> Social Services
> Education
> Leisure
> Environmental Health

9.30 In districts where the substantial redevelopment and refurbishing of an outworn area is a major problem, it would be possible to argue that the development and housing functions are so interrelated that they should both be within the sphere of responsibility of one committee. Generally speaking, however, we would envisage separate committees and the structure illustrated in Diagram 4(a) reflects this view.

9.31 The major functions allocated to the six committees are:

Education	Education
	Libraries *
	Museums *
	Art Galleries *

* *Could alternatively be placed under Recreation and Amenities*

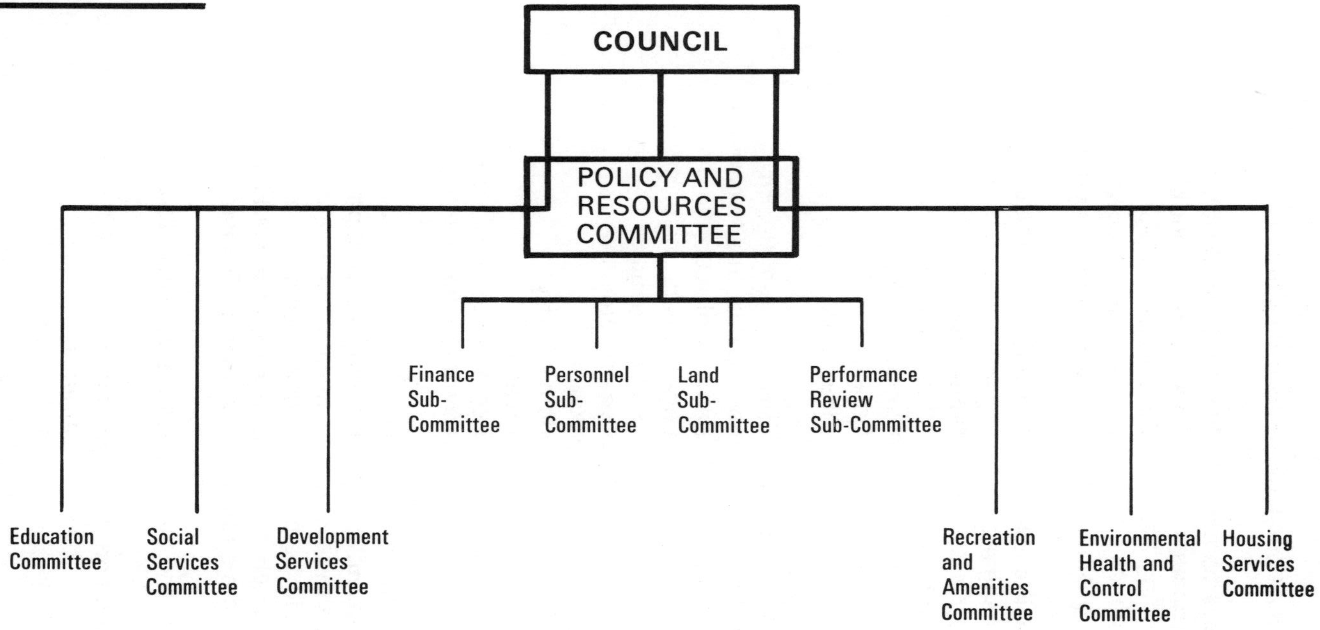

Diagram 4(a) — Committee structure — Metropolitan district

COUNCIL

POLICY AND RESOURCES COMMITTEE

Education Committee

Social Services Committee

Development Services Committee

Finance Sub-Committee

Personnel Sub-Committee

Land Sub-Committee

Performance Review Sub-Committee

Recreation and Amenities Committee

Environmental Health and Control Committee

Housing Services Committee

Social Services	Social Services
Development Services	Planning and Development Development Control Derelict Land Clearance Building Regulations Highways and Footways
Recreation and Amenities	Recreation and Tourism Entertainments Commons Allotments Country Parks Caravan Sites Gipsy Sites
Environmental Health and Control	Environmental Health Food Safety and Hygiene Refuse Collection Local Sewers Land Drainage Coast Protection Litter Home Safety Clean Air Registration and Licensing Health Education Markets

Housing Services	Housing Management
	    Maintenance
	    Improvement
	    Assessment of Needs
	    Advisory Service
	Slum Clearance
	House Purchase Loans

9.32 The departmental structure follows broadly the same pattern as that shown in earlier diagrams for the non-metropolitan county.

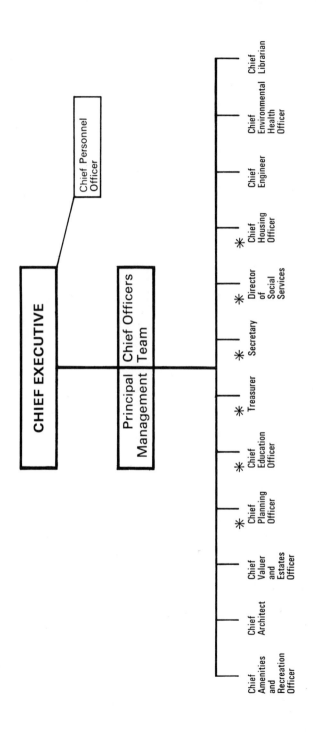

CHIEF EXECUTIVE

Chief Personnel Officer

Principal Management Team

Chief Officers Team

Chief Amenities and Recreation Officer

Chief Architect

Chief Valuer and Estates Officer

* Chief Planning Officer

* Chief Education Officer

* Treasurer

* Secretary

* Director of Social Services

* Chief Housing Officer

Chief Engineer

Chief Environmental Health Officer

Chief Librarian

* Members of management team.

Diagram 4(b) — Departmental structure A — Metropolitan district

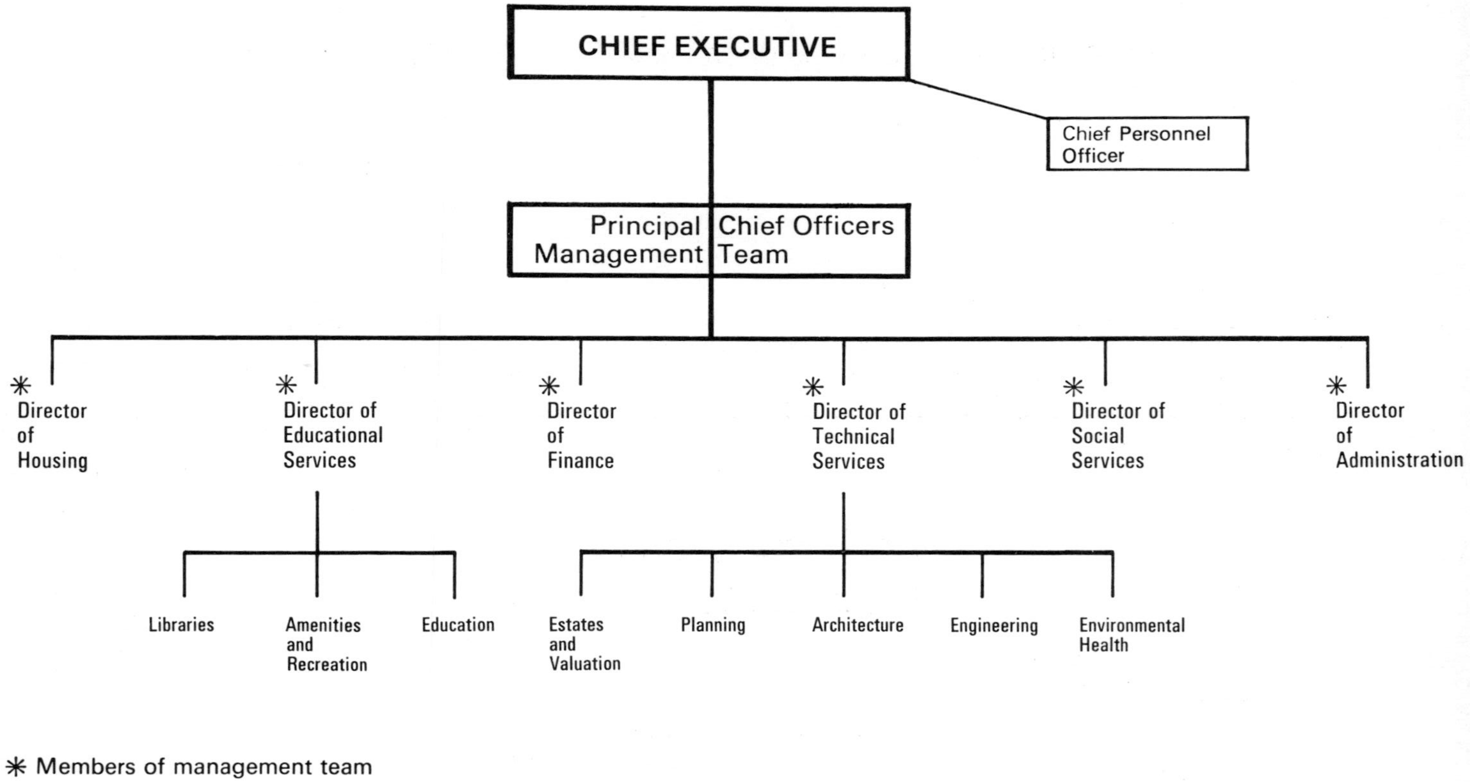

Diagram 4(c) — Departmental structure B — Metropolitan district

* Members of management team

Diagram 4(b) illustrates the type of structure likely to be appropriate where there is no grouping of departments under directors and Diagram 4(c) shows a 'directorate' structure. The comments which we made in paragraphs 9.16 and 9.17 apply equally to this diagram.

9.33 We believe that the Chief Housing Officer (Diagram 4(b)) and the Director of Housing (Diagram 4(c)) should in each case be responsible for the total housing function, including management, assessment of need, improvement, slum clearance and any advisory service. In order to carry out these functions they would use the services of the appropriate specialist officers of other departments.

The Non-Metropolitan District

9.34 The allocation of functions to non-metropolitan districts suggests that there might be either three or four programme committees. In the ordinary way we can see a logical division into three programmes but the size and/or special characteristics of some districts suggest that four committees might be required. An additional committee may be required in those districts which will retain responsibility for existing passenger transport undertakings.

9.35 In Diagram 5(a) we illustrate a possible committee structure containing three committees. In that structure the allocation of main functions between the committees is:

Housing Services	Housing Management Maintenance Improvement Assessment of Future Need Advisory Service Slum Clearance House Purchase Loans	
Development/ Leisure Services	Local Plans and Development Development Control Land Use Derelict Land Building Regulations	Development

115

	Recreation & Tourism Entertainments Museums Commons	Leisure & Recreation
Environmental Health & Control	Highways Litter Coast Protection Land Drainage Markets Home Safety Licensing & Registration	Control/Protection
	Food Safety & Hygiene Refuse Collection Local Sewers Clean Air Noise Nuisances Offensive Trades Health Education Pollution Control Cemeteries & Mortuaries Conveniences	Health

9.36 In this structure it is suggested that there might be established two working groups of members for each of the programme committees. The two areas of activity in the Housing Services Committee might, for example, be the public and private aspects of housing. In the other two committees the areas of activity are as shown in the list of functions in the preceding paragraph.

9.37 In the alternative structure in Diagram 5(b) the major difference would be the creation of a separate Recreation and Amenities Committee and the allocation of the highways and litter control functions to the Development Services Committee.

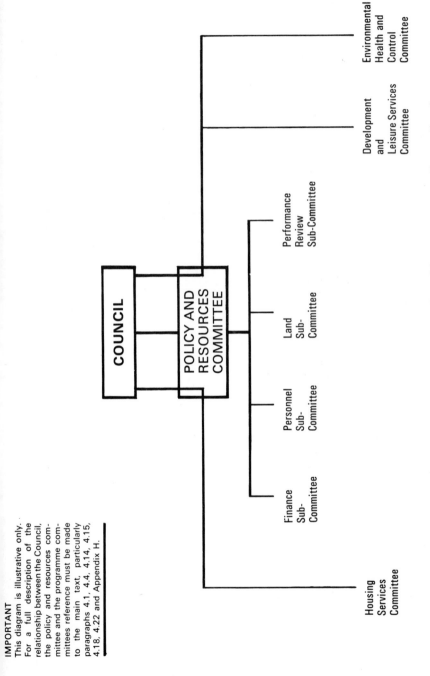

COUNCIL

POLICY AND RESOURCES COMMITTEE

Finance Sub-Committee

Personnel Sub-Committee

Land Sub-Committee

Performance Review Sub-Committee

Housing Services Committee

Development and Leisure Services Committee

Environmental Health and Control Committee

Diagram 5(a) — Committee structure A — Non-metropolitan district

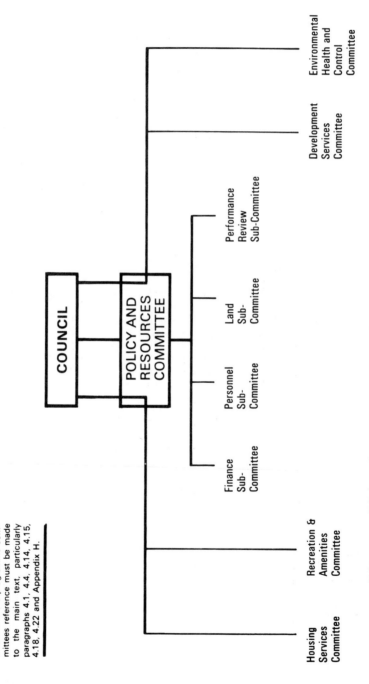

COUNCIL

POLICY AND RESOURCES COMMITTEE

Finance Sub-Committee

Personnel Sub-Committee

Land Sub-Committee

Performance Review Sub-Committee

Housing Services Committee

Recreation & Amenities Committee

Development Services Committee

Environmental Health and Control Committee

Diagram 5(b) — Committee structure B — Non-metropolitan district

9.38 At departmental level we feel that there are a number of possible permutations, because of the wide range in size and type of district. We are agreed that each district will require the following officers:—

Chief Executive
Chief Housing Officer
Chief Environmental Health Officer
Treasurer (or Chief Financial Officer)
Secretary

9.39 In addition districts will require some or all of the following skills:—

Architecture
Engineering
Estates and Valuation
Law
Planning

and in some of the larger districts it may be necessary for each to be represented by a Chief Officer heading his own department. In others it may be that there will be scope for the dually-qualified man to head a department combining two skills and in yet others the requirement may depend upon the arrangements made between district and county for the discharge of particular functions. Some districts may find it convenient to use the services of private practitioners.

9.40 Such is the wide variety in the size and nature of districts that it may be necessary to appoint other Chief Officers, like Passenger Transport Manager or Chief Amenities and Recreation Officer. Diagram 5(c) represents the position in the largest districts. In Diagram 5(d) which might represent medium sized and smaller districts, the general structure is very similar, but a Chief Technical Officer heads a department in which all design and construction work and the management of the authority's labour force might be located, together with various other appropriate services.

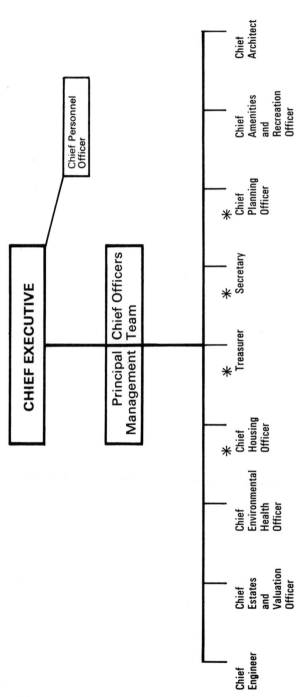

CHIEF EXECUTIVE

Chief Personnel Officer

Principal Chief Officers Management Team

Chief Engineer

Chief Estates and Valuation Officer

Chief Environmental Health Officer

* Chief Housing Officer

* Treasurer

* Secretary

* Chief Planning Officer

Chief Amenities and Recreation Officer

Chief Architect

* Members of management team. Local circumstances may justify additional members.

Diagram 5(c) — Departmental structure — Larger non-metropolitan district

Note : In appropriate authorities the Passenger Transport Manager may also be a chief officer.

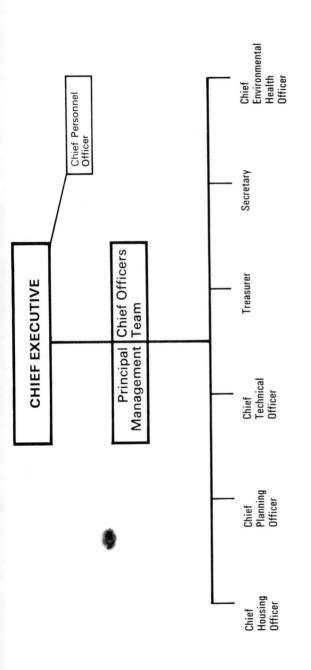

Diagram 5(d) — Departmental structure — Average non-metropolitan district

Note: In view of the relatively small number of departments, all chief officers will probably be members of the management team.

Main points of the report

This report does not readily summarise, but as many who have read will wish to have a summary for reference purposes, the following a list of the main points. It must be emphasised that the full meaning of these brief extracts cannot be appreciated except in the context of the report as a whole.

Chapter 2 Local Government management—its nature and purpose

1 The management structures of many local authorities remain those which emerged from the development of local government in the 19th century. Reorganisation provides a unique opportunity for critical self examination and change. (para. 2.)

2 There is no one perfect system of management in local government any more than in any other sphere of activity. (para. 2.4)

3 The dual nature of management in local government must be recognised. (para. 2.6)

4 Local government is not limited to the provision of services. is concerned with the overall economic, cultural and physical well being of the community. (para. 2.10)

5 The traditional departmental attitude within much of local government must give way to a wider ranging corporate outlook. (para. 2.11)

6 Management is not an end in itself. Changes in management structure must be justified in terms of the benefit to the community. (para. 2.13)

1   In a highly labour intensive organisation like local government the major scope for improvements in efficiency and effectiveness must come through more effective use of human resources.   (para. 6.2)

2   The human problems of management in local government are in no way different from those in industry or other areas of the public service, but local government lags behind in its recognition and development of the personnel management function.   (para. 6.14)

3   Personnel management and management services should be separate in the structure of a local authority, with coordination exercised at a high level.   (para. 6.19)

4   The traditional 'Establishment' title should be dropped in favour of the more widely recognised title 'personnel management'.
                                                                                 (para. 6.21)

5   The status of the head of the personnel department must be improved from that which he now occupies. He should have direct access to the Chief Executive and not be subordinated to any other chief officer.   (para. 6.34)

6   Chief officers in other departments will be expected to accept and act on the advice of the personnel officer on matters within his specialised knowledge in exactly the same way as they would normally accept the Treasurer's advice on financial matters.   (para. 6.36)

Chapter 7 Other central functions

1   'Management services' is a term which embraces all "services which help management to plan, control and improve the activities of the organisation in a general sense". It is not limited to O & M and and Work Study.   (para. 7.5)

2   Services to management may validly reside in various places and do not necessarily require to be administered within one monolithic management services unit. Some techniques may be most effectively utilised by placing them within individual departments though others will, by their nature, require to be centrally administered.   (para. 7.20)

3 Wherever the relevant specialists are located, there is increasing scope for teams from various departments contributing to the examination and appraisal of projects under consideration by the management team. (para. 7.21)

4 The effectiveness of management services must be subject to the same critical examination as that of the departments which they service. **(para. 7.23)**

5 Control of computer time and facilities should be exercised by a body separate from the department in which the computer is situated. That body should be responsible direct to the management team.
(para. 7.10)

6 In order that any corporate planning unit may be kept in touch with the reality of what is actually happening 'on the ground' it should involve officers from the various departments of the authority directly in the corporate planning process and not be staffed by 'professional' corporate planners. (para. 7.28)

7 The larger authorities should set up a full-time public relations and information unit headed by a suitably qualified officer. The duty to provide information should not only be recognised, but should be demonstrated. (para. 7.38)

8 Authorities should consider the publication of an annual report to the electorate, containing not only factual information about the utilisation of the authority's resources, but an identification of problems and needs and of plans for meeting them. (para. 7.39)

9 Staff must be kept fully informed on all matters which have, or are believed to have, a direct bearing upon them. (para. 7.41)

10 Each authority should create and maintain a central record of all land and buildings within its ownership. The economic use of existing property should be subject to continuous reappraisal and review.
(para. 7.49 and 7.50)

11 Members should be provided with adequate secretarial services to assist with their Council and constituency duties. (para. 7.50 and 7.52)

Chapter 8 Working arrangements between the new authorities—the "community" approach

1   In the interests of the community as a whole, local authorities must, in the future, establish a closer working relationship both with each other and with other bodies, than has generally been the case in the past. This will apply particularly to the new area health and regional water authorities.   (para. 8.4)

2   A district joint committee consisting of both district and county members should be set up for each district to co-ordinate the interaction of county and district functions and policies for the locality. (para. 8.6)

3   A county joint committee, consisting of representatives of the county council and of each of the districts within the county, should be created to provide a forum for the joint planning of the broad overall policies of the county and its constituent districts. (para. 8.11)

4   At officer level there should be regular and formal meetings between officers at county and district level. Joint meetings of the management teams of the county and either individual districts or small groups of districts should also be considered.   (para. 8.14)

5   Authorities will each have skills, information and resources which others will lack and arrangements should be made to ensure that they are made available to those other authorities.   (para. 8.15 and 8.16)

Appendix A

Interim report of the Working Group

I   Introduction

1   You asked us to report to you by the middle of September on any matters within our terms of reference on which we thought our views would be helpful to the Government while they are still preparing the legislation on local government reorganisation.

2   It seemed to us that there were two questions we should set out to answer.

> (i)   Which existing statutory provisions would be likely to hinder the new authorities from being good managers if they were re-enacted?

> (ii)   What new statutory powers would be likely to help the new authorities to be good managers?

3   Underlying our approach to these questions was the belief that the new authorities will be responsible and competent and should be treated accordingly.

4   In answering the questions we have asked ourselves what is best from the point of view of local authority management. We recognise that there may be other relevant considerations—for example, of a constitutional nature. But they are outside our terms of reference and we have not attempted to deal with them.

5   The timetable we were given for the preparation of our interim report was very short. July and August are the months in which many people are on holiday. For these reasons we have not been able to collect evidence on the questions we asked ourselves. Nor have we been able to discuss them with the members of our expert panels or anyone else. There was not time to do so if we were to report by mid-September. If there is anything in the evidence we shall be receiving which leads us to modify any of our proposals in this, our interim report, we shall tell you immediately.

II Existing statutory provisions

6 Our first question was: which existing statutory provisions would be likely to hinder the new authorities from being good managers if they were re-enacted?

7 All the provisions we have examined affect the way local authorities organise their work at member and officer levels. Some have a very significant effect; others have little consequence.

8 The existing statutory requirements concerned are of four kinds:

> (a) the requirements on local authorities to appoint certain separate committees (eg county finance committees);
>
> (b) the Ministerial controls over the appointment of certain officers (eg chief education officers);
>
> (c) Ministerial controls over the dismissal of certain officers (eg clerks of county councils);
>
> (d) the requirements on local authorities to appoint certain specified officers (eg town clerks and treasurers).

9 We have concluded that there are four fundamental objections to. such provisions. We deal with the most important objection last; the other three objections are in no particular order.

10 First, the existing provisions are neither logical nor consistent. It is not logical, for example, to lay down provisions about the committees and officers for some vital services (eg education, social services) but not for others which are equally vital (eg housing and planning). Nor is it consistent to require county councils, for example, to have a separate finance committee but not to impose a similar duty on other authorities. We were left with the impression that many of the existing provisions had been enacted because individual services had been looked at in isolation, not in the context of the total activities of a local authority.

11   Second, we have not come across any evidence in our experience as local government officers which would suggest that services which are subject to controls over committees and officers are better administered than services which are not affected by such controls.

12   Third, we believe that the existing statutory provisions result in a rigid framework, set up for reasons and in circumstances which are not now valid. They thus inhibit the adoption of management structures which would suit the current needs of individual authorities and hinder the introduction of new management techniques, which, for their best utilisation, often require fresh approaches to structure and management.

13   Fourth, and most important, the present statutory provisions encourage "departmentalism". By this, we mean individual committees and departments behaving as though they are independent of the council and each other. The local authority itself and not its committees, is responsible for the provision of services. Departmentalism, which is bolstered up by the present law, hampers authorities from assessing the problems of their areas comprehensively and deciding priorities not merely within each service but also between services. As a result it can lead to waste of resources, friction between one member or officer and another and weak administrative control. It can cause poor co-operation between departments leading to delays in finding solutions to problems. It permits situations to arise in which the right hand does not know what the left hand is doing.

14   With these general comments as the background, the next three sections of the interim report look in detail at the existing statutory provisions affecting first, committee organisation; second, the appointment and dismissal of certain officers; and third, the appointment of certain named officers. In section VI we recommend what new statutory powers would be likely to be helpful and section VII contains our general conclusions.

III Committees

15 At present the relevant local authorities are required by law to appoint the following separate committees:

(a) **Health**—section 19(3) and Part II, 4th Schedule, National Health Service Act 1946;

(b) **Social Services**—section 2, Local Authority Social Services Act 1970;

(c) **Education**—Part II, 1st Schedule, Education Act 1944;

(d) **Finance**—(county councils only)—section 86, Local Government Act 1933;

(e) **Allotments**—section 14, Allotments Act 1922;

(f) **Diseases of Animals**—section 60 and 4th Schedule, Diseases of Animals Act 1950;

(g) **Public Health and Housing**—(county councils only)— section 156, Housing Act 1957;

(h) **Police or Watch**—section 2, Police Act 1964;

(i) **National Parks**—section 8(3), National Parks and Access to the Countryside Act 1948;

(j) **Youth Employment sub-committee**—section 10(2), Employment and Training Act 1948.

16 These requirements may have originated from a wish to ensure that authorities devoted sufficient attention to the service concerned or to foster the development of a new service. We feel confident that when most of the requirements were enacted, the effect of the requirement on the overall organisation of local authorities was not considered. It will be clear from what we have said in paragraphs 10 to 13 that we believe that this sort of piece-meal approach is mistaken. Moreover, we do not consider that a service can develop fully if it is artificially isolated from other related services.

17 There are special constitutional provisions relating to the composition of police (or watch) committees and committees dealing with national parks. The law requires that one-third of the members of police and watch committees should be magistrates and that the Secretary of State should appoint one-third of the members of national parks' committees. It is not within our terms of reference to express an opinion on the desirability of these special provisions about the membership of the two committees. It should be recognised, however, that these special provisions will inhibit a free and unfettered approach to management structures, the desirability of which is clear from what we have said in paragraphs 10 to 13.

18 We do not accept that the requirement to appoint a social services committee is essential to give successful effect to the Seebohm Committee's report and to ensure the proper development of the local authority personal social services. The proposal for a separate committee was only one of the many Seebohm recommendations about the service and we do not believe that the implementation of all the others depends upon that one. There is, in any event, no question of the present requirement being removed before 1 April 1974; by that time the service will surely have become firmly established. We are inclined to think that the retention of the requirement after that date could be detrimental to the service itself. It could lead to the isolation of the social services from closely related services and thus could inhibit their full development. Moreover, the removal of the requirement would not prevent authorities from having a separate social services committee and department. But it would permit authorities to adopt alternative arrangements if they were more appropriate to their needs.

19 The education service is one of the most firmly established and highly developed local government services. We believe that the service would be in no way adversely affected if the statutory requirement to appoint an education committee were removed.

20 In paragraphs 10 to 13 we listed four objections to controls over the internal organisation of local authorities. We have found nothing in our study of the requirements listed in paragraph 15 which makes us want to modify these objections. We recognise the importance of the services concerned and the need for them to be given all the attention and resources they need. We consider, however, that this can be achieved without the requirements to appoint special committees. Far from adversely affecting the services concerned, we believe that the removal of these controls would permit a more sensitive and flexible organisation which would be in the interests of the services themselves and the people for whom they are provided. We accordingly recommend that none of the present statutory requirements to appoint certain specified committees should be retained—either temporarily or permanently—after reorganisation.

IV The appointment and dismissal of certain officers

21 Ministerial approval is required in connection with the appointment of: *

<blockquote>

(a)   chief constables, deputy and assistant chief constables;

(b)   chief education officers;

(c)   directors of social services;

(d)   chief fire officers;

(e)   public analysts.

</blockquote>

In some cases the Minister's consent is required to the appointment of the candidate himself and in other cases to the short list of candidates from whom the local authority may make the final appointment.

22   These controls were probably introduced with the aim of ensuring that men and women with the necessary personal qualities and qualifications were appointed to assist local authorities with the provision of important services. Alternatively, some may have been based on the wish to avoid any possibility or suggestion of local partiality in filling posts.

* *The Ministerial controls over the appointment of agricultural analysts, deputy analysts and inspectors and samplers under the Fertilisers and Feeding Stuffs Act 1926 will lapse when the Agriculture Act 1970 comes into effect.*

23   The objectives underlying these controls are, of course, as valid now as on the day they were introduced. We believe, however, that the objectives can be achieved without making appointments subject to Ministerial approval. This is evident from the fact that local authorities have chosen suitable candidates to fill key posts over which no controls exist (eg town clerks, treasurers, housing managers) and have not shown partiality in making appointments. The existence of the controls is, moreover, contributory to the attitude of "departmentalism" which we discussed in paragraph 13.

24   We have given special consideration to the control over the appointment of chief constables and deputy and assistant chief constables. Their role and duties are in many respects different from those of other senior officers in local government. Nonetheless, we consider on grounds of good local authority management that the controls over their appointment should not continue. We recognise, however, that these posts have exceptional characteristics which the Government will need to take into account. Those special considerations are outside the scope of our work; therefore, we cannot comment on them. We are satisfied, however, that special considerations of a comparable nature do not exist in the case of the other posts listed in paragraph 21 and we are in no doubt that the Ministerial controls over those appointments should not be retained.

25   The dismissal of an officer from the following posts is subject to Ministerial control:

> (a)   chief constables, deputy and assistant chief constables;
>
> (b)   clerks of county councils;
>
> (c)   medical officers of health;
>
> (d)   senior public health inspectors under section 110 of the Local Government Act 1933;
>
> (e)   public analysts;
>
> (f)   inspectors under the Diseases of Animals Act 1950.

26 We could deduce no coherent principle on which it was decided to make dismissal from these posts and only these, subject to Ministerial control. We considered, therefore, not only whether these controls should be retained but also whether the dismissal of all senior officers should be subject to Ministerial confirmation.

27 The case for such controls seems to be that unless senior officers are given the protection of Ministerial control, they may be afraid to speak their minds for fear of being dismissed by their employing council

28 If that is the rationale we do not, of course, dispute the thought which underlies it. Officers should give their councils advice without fear or favour, even if they know that in doing so they will make themselves unpopular. Indeed, we consider that an officer would fail in his duty if he did not do so.

29 We cannot agree, however, that officers need protection before they will give the proper advice. Town clerks, treasurers, housing managers and the other senior officers whose posts are not subject to Ministerial control are not, in our experience, less willing to do their duty than those whose posts are subject to control.

30 We do not accept the implication behind the Ministerial control ie that authorities will unreasonably dismiss their staff. If it is feared that councils cannot be trusted to behave reasonably in this respect then local authorities cannot at the same time be regarded as the right bodies to provide the wide and important services for which Parliament has made them responsible.

31 There is a further and very practical consideration. If a council decides to dismiss one of its officers, the relationship of trust and confidence which is essential between them will have broken down. If the Minister concerned declined to confirm the dismissal, that would not repair the damage. The officer's effectiveness would have been reduced and the work for which he was responsible would suffer as a result. It would not be in the interests of the officer himself, the council or—above all—the public for him to continue in his post in such circumstances.

32 We have again given special thought to the position of chief constables and deputy and assistant chief constables. What we have said in the preceding three paragraphs applies equally to them; however, they are also officers of the Crown. This special constitutional consideration may make it necessary for the Home Secretary's control over the dismissal of these officers to be retained.

33 We are satisfied, however, that exceptional considerations of this sort do not apply to the other posts listed in paragraph 25. We recommend, therefore, that for the reasons given in paragraphs 29 to 31 the Ministerial controls over the dismissal of clerks of county councils, medical officers of health, senior public health inspectors, public analysts and inspectors under the Diseases of Animals Act 1950 should not be retained. Implicit in our recommendation is the belief that councillors and officers can be relied upon to behave in a reasonable and responsible manner.

34 While recommending the removal of all central control over the appointment and dismissal of officers, there is one ancillary matter to which we attach importance. Under the law as it now stands, an officer whose services are terminated receives nothing other than a refund of his superannuation contributions even though he may be within only a short period of reaching his normal retiring age. We strongly recommend that where an officer's services are terminated he should at the very least have his accrued superannuation rights "frozen" until he reaches retiring age. Furthermore, there may be cases where an officer's mental or physical condition is such that his efficiency has dropped below standards which are acceptable to his authority. His condition may nevertheless not be such as to qualify him for a permanent ill-health pension. We strongly recommend that consideration should be given to legislation enabling a local authority to pay a pension to an officer in such circumstances provided he is nearing the retiring age. Provision on these lines has already been made in a number of local Acts; we recommend that it should be made general. We understand that the Commissioners of Inland Revenue do not consider that such a pension should be payable more than ten years before the normal retiring age (ie 55 in the case of the Local Government Scheme or 50 in the case of the Civil Service). On management grounds, however, we believe that the pension should be payable from the age of 50 and that the qualifying age should be fixed by reference to age, not by reference to the normal retiring age for any particular scheme. We accordingly recommend that the Commissioners should review their policy in order to enable such pensions to be paid to local government officers who have attained the age of 50.

V Requirements to appoint certain named officers

35 The statutes at present require local authorities to appoint the following named officers: clerks of county and county district councils; town clerks; treasurers; surveyors; medical officers of health; public health inspectors; weights and measures inspectors; chief fire officers; chief education officers; directors of social services; chief constables; mental welfare officers; architects (London boroughs only); inspectors under the Pharmacy and Poisons Act 1933, the Fertilisers and Feeding Stuffs Act 1926, the Agriculture Act 1970 and the Diseases of Animals Act 1950; agricultural analysts and deputy analysts; public analysts; accountants and mechanicians under the Betting, Gaming and Lotteries Act 1963.

36 Many of these requirements exercise a significant effect on local authority management structures. They encourage "departmentalism"; it is often assumed that because the officer is named in the statute he should have his own independent department and report to his own separate committee.

37 No doubt the objective when these requirements were introduced was to ensure that all authorities appointed a competent and identifiable officer to deal with the service concerned.

38 Of course the new authorities must appoint the necessary staff if they are to do their work properly. We certainly agree that they should establish clear and unambiguous lines of accountability at officer level; for example, it is vital that in each authority there should be an officer who is easily identifiable and is fully answerable for the council's financial affairs.

39 But we do not accept that it is necessary to specify in law all the officers which local authorities should employ. It is evident that the existing authorities do appoint the officers they require without any statutory prompting. Nor do we believe that the requirement to appoint an officer necessarily results in fully accountable management. We are aware of nothing which would support the view that officers whose appointment is not a statutory requirement are less accountable than those whose appointments are required. On the other hand, we do believe that the present legal provisions can hamper the establishment of rational management structures which suit local circumstances. We set out the objections to such provisions in paragraphs 10 to 13 above.

40 There are, however, a handful of posts which authorities are required to fill and which demand highly specialised skills or knowledge outside the normal scope of local government. Such posts are often filled on a part-time basis, eg by firms of consultants. The posts concerned are agricultural analysts, deputy agricultural analysts and accountants and mechanicians under the Betting, Gaming and Lotteries Act 1963. They exercise little or no influence on management structures and we would not press for the present requirements to be repealed.

41 We recommend, however, that all the other statutory requirements listed in paragraph 34 should not be retained.

VI New Powers

42 The second question we set out to answer was: what new statutory powers would be likely to help the new authorities to be good managers?

43 We started from the view that good management is not something for which one can legislate. But, on the other hand, local authorities are, of course, creatures of statute which do all their work within a statutory framework. We looked at the present framework, therefore, and asked how it could be improved. We decided that there is one new general power which would be useful to the new authorities.

44 First, we think that the present legal doubts about the power of local authorities to delegate to their officers should be removed. There are, of course, some things that a council would not and ought not to leave to its officers to decide—for example, major policy decisions, the allocation of resources and, of course, the decision about what rate or precept to charge. We soon came to the conclusion, however, that it is not practicable to draw up a comprehensive list of matters which might be delegated and another list of matters which should never be delegated. A question which may fall within clearly decided policies and may not raise any delicate issues in one area may be very sensitive in another area. Indeed, the same question may be a straightforward matter of administration at one time but may become a matter of major policy at some other time within one area.

45   It is clear, however, that if the best use is to be made of members' and officers' time and abilities, the former must be willing to delegate where appropriate and the latter should be willing to accept the responsibility. We also think that members should not hesitate to tell officers when they consider that a matter which has been delegated should in future, or in a particular case, be decided by the council, a committee or a sub-committee. Similarly, an officer should not hesitate to ask elected members to decide a matter if he thinks it raises particularly important or sensitive questions outside his competence.

46   What is needed, therefore, is a general power which enables the elected members and their officers in each authority to work out flexible and rational schemes of organisation and delegation, whether or not based on a committee structure. For the reasons given in paragraph 44, we do not believe it to be practicable to specify a list of what may or may not be delegated in all circumstances. We recommend, therefore, that the power of the new local authorities to delegate to their members and officers—either individually or collectively—should be as wide as the power of the existing local authorities to delegate to their committees under section 85 of the Local Government Act 1933.

47   We further recommend that each authority should set a time limit on its scheme of delegation. At the end of the period (eg 12 months), the council or committee should consider, in discussion with the officers concerned, how the scheme has worked and whether it requires modification. We do not think it sensible to say what the time limit on schemes should be and we certainly consider that it would be wrong to prescribe the period in the statute. Each authority should decide its own time limit—in some circumstances it might be as little as six months and in others a few years. No doubt councils which are elected for a three or four year term would want to review the existing delegation scheme soon after the election. We consider it essential that at regular intervals members and officers should discuss the delegation schemes and that members should then take a positive decision about what to devolve.

VII   Conclusions

48   Our recommendations are designed to pave the way for a new approach to local authority management. We believe that the removal of the existing statutory constraints is an essential precondition if the new authorities are to have rational management structures which are suited to local needs, which make the best use of resources and which provide the public with developing services of a high standard. We do not believe that the removal of the controls would adversely effect any of the services or the staff concerned. On the contrary we believe they would benefit from the greater freedom and the wider scope that would be open to them.

49   At the same time we are conscious of the fact that if the new authorities have greater freedom, the need for both elected members and officers to give positive, rational and sustained attention to management will be correspondingly greater. We shall prepare the advice in our final report with this in mind.

Signed   M A Bains (Chairman)
                  J E Bolton
                  H D Jeffries
                  J V Miller
                  G C Moore
                  R G Morgan
                              E B C Osmotherly (Secretary)
                              D A McDonald (Assistant Secretary)

16 September 1971

Addendum to the Interim Report

1 On 26 August the Department of the Environment circulated to the local authority associations and other interested bodies a consultation paper on statutory provisions affecting the internal organisation of local authorities in England and Wales. By that stage we had reached agreement on all our main points and recommendations and were well advanced with the preparation of our interim report.

2 There is much in the consultation paper which accords with our recommendations. There are, however, several proposals in the paper with which we disagree and the purpose of this Addendum is to draw attention to them.

3 First, as we have said in paragraph 17 of the interim report, it should be recognised that the special provisions affecting police and national parks committees inhibit a free and unfettered approach to management structures, the desirability of which we have referred to in paragraphs 10 to 13 above (see paragraph 7 of the consultation paper).

4 Second, we have explained in paragraph 18 of our report, why we do not accept the need to retain the requirement to appoint a separate social services committee (paragraph 8 of the consultation paper). We believe that the retention of the requirement would be in the interests of neither the social services themselves nor the management of local government generally.

5 Third, paragraph 9 of the consultation paper gives no explanation of the Government's proposal initially to retain the requirement to appoint an education committee. We see no reason, therefore, to modify the view expressed in paragraph 19 of our report.

6 Nor do paragraphs 18 and 19 of the consultation paper explain why it is proposed to retain the existing Ministerial controls over the appointment and/or dismissal of chief constables, deputy and assistant chief constables, chief fire officers and directors of social services. Our views on the controls affecting these senior police officers are set out in paragraphs 24 and 32 of the interim report and paragraphs 22 and 23 apply to chief fire officers and directors of social services.

7 Our views on paragraph 13 of the consultation paper will be clear from section V of the interim report. In particular, we do not understand why the requirement to appoint a chief inspector and other inspectors of weights and measures cannot be removed even if the Department of Trade and Industry remains responsible for the relevant professional examinations.

8 The consultation paper does not deal with the superannuation position of officers whose services are terminated. It is, however, a matter to which we have referred in paragraph 34 of the interim report; the provisions we have recommended are desirable on management grounds.

9 Finally, we have no objection to the proposal in paragraph 21 of the consultation paper. But, as we have said in paragraph 46 of the interim report, we recommend that the powers of the new authorities should be sufficiently wide and flexible for each one to delegate to its members and officers—either individually or collectively—in the way best suited to its own circumstances.

Signed   M A Bains
               J E Bolton
               H D Jeffries
               J V Miller
               G C Moore
               R G Morgan

                         E B C Osmotherly (Secretary)
                         D A McDonald (Assistant Secretary)

16 September 1971

Appendix B

Written evidence
list of witnesses

Organisations

Architects and Surveyors, Incorporated Association of

Archivists, Society of

British Newspaper Editors, Guild of

Burial and Cremation, Institute of

Chief Fire Officers' Association

Chief Officer Group of Engineers and Surveyors in the proposed New Hertfordshire District Authority No 1

City Engineers' Group

Civil Defence Officers, Association of

Clerks of County District Councils, Society of

Clerks of the Peace of Counties and of Clerks of County Councils, Society of (now called Society of County Clerks)

Confederation of British Industry

County Architects' Society and City and Borough Architects' Society
(joint submission)

County Borough Chief Quantity Surveyors, Society of

County Borough Treasurers, Society of

County Civil Defence Officers' Society

County Librarians, Society of

County Planning Officers' Society

County Public Health Officers, Association of

County Surveyors' Society

County Treasurers' Society

Directors of Social Services, Association of

Education Committees, Association of

Education Officers, Society of

Greater London Council Staff Association

Greater London and South East Sports Council

Health Visitors' Association

Housing Managers, Institute of

Labour Party

Leicester Polytechnic

Local Authority Valuers and Estate Agents, Association of

Local Government Administrators, Institute of

Local Government Engineers and Surveyors, Association of

Local Government Financial Officers, Association of

Local Government Group of the Institute of Public Relations

Local Government Personnel and Management Services Group

Local Government Personnel and Management Services Group No 2 (South Wales, South West and Western England)

Local Government Training Board

London Boroughs' Association

London Boroughs' Management Services Unit

Management Consultants Association Ltd

Master Builders, Federation of

McKinsey and Co Inc

Municipal Building Management, Institute of

Municipal Engineers, Institution of

Municipal Treasurers and Accountants, Institute of

Museums Association and Society of Museum Officers (joint submission)

National and Local Government Officers' Association

National Association of Divisional Executives for Education

National Association of Fire Officers

National Association of Inspectors of Schools and Educational Organisers

National Association of Youth Service Officers

National Building Agency

National Corporation for the Care of Old People

National Joint Committee of Working Women's Organisations

National Union of Conservative and Unionist Associations

National Union of Teachers

Operational Research, Institute for

Operational Research Society Ltd

P A Management Consultants Ltd

Park and Recreation Administration, Institute of

P E Consulting Group Ltd

Private Architects, Association of

Public Analysts, Association of

Public Cleansing, Institute of

Public Health Inspectors, Association of and Public Health Inspectors, Guild of (joint submission)

Public Services Group of the London and South East Region of the Institute of Personnel Management

Purchasing and Supply, Institute of

Quantity Surveyors, Institute of

Road Safety Officers, Institute of

Royal Institute of British Architects

Royal Institution of Chartered Surveyors

Royal Town Planning Institute

Sheffield Polytechnic—Unit for Management in the Public Services

Surrey Chief Public Health Inspectors, Society of

Town Clerks, Society of

Town and Country Planning Association

Trades Union Congress

Urwick, Orr and Partners Ltd

Water Engineers, Institute of

Weights and Measures, Institute of

West Hertfordshire Main Drainage Authority

Appendix B /contd.

Individuals

Mr S R Barnes

Professor B Benjamin, PHD FIA

Mr P J Blackmore, BA

Mr V A Butler MA

Mr A G Dawtry, CBE, TD, LLB

Mr C H Fairman

Mr J H W Glen, LLB

Mr P Graham

Mr W A Hampton, B.Sc(Econ), PH.D

Mr C A Howard-Luck, DMA, DCA

Mr K Hughes, DMA

Mr M A Large, MAPHI, MRSH

Mr F B W Linnitt

Mr J Mann, MA

Mr J C Maxwell

Mr C F May, DPA, ARICS, MIMunE, AMBIM

Mr R H McCall, OBE

Mr V H Mellor, DPA(LOND)

Mr A W Miles, MA

Mr R S Parsons, DMA, MIPR

Mr R C Rees, MA, LLB

Mr F C Roberts

Mr W W Ruff, DL

Mr S Sami, BA, BCD, PFTArb.

Mr B Scholes, MA, LAMTPI

Mr E G Sibert MTPI, FRICS

Mr E J Skevington, DMA, MILGA, jointly with Mr B A Barker, DMA, MILGA, Mr N M Swinney DMA, MILGA, and Mr R J Wager, BA (Cantab), MSc, Assoc Member ILGA

Mr J Skitt, FInst PC

Councillor Mrs M B Simey, BA, JP

Mr W E Templeton, MInstWPC, MIPHE

Mr J B Woodham, BSc (Econ) FIMTA

Government Departments

Department of Education and Science

Department of the Environment

Welsh Office

Appendix C

List of local authorities submitting written evidence

Basildon Urban District Council

Blaby Rural District Council

Bolton County Borough Council

Bournemouth County Borough Council

Cardiff County Borough Council

Chelmsford Rural District Council

Coventry County Borough Council

Crawley Urban District Council

Derbyshire County Council

Ealing London Borough Council

Easthampstead Rural District Council

Gelligaer Urban District Council

Greenwich London Borough Council

Grimsby County Borough Council

Grimsby Rural District Council

Haringey London Borough Council

Havant and Waterloo Urban District Council

Leeds County Borough Council

Liverpool County Borough Council

Malling Rural District Council

Monmouth Borough Council

Newcastle upon Tyne County Borough Council

Newton Abbot Rural District Council

Northumberland County Council

Redditch Urban District Council

Seaton Valley Urban District Council
Stockport County Borough Council
Strood Rural District Council
Swindon Borough Council
Teesside County Borough Council
Walton and Weybridge Urban District Council
Winsford Urban District Council
Woking Urban District Council

Appendix D

Local Authorities visited by members of the Working Group

Name of Authority	Date of visit
Gloucestershire County Council	2 December 1971
London Borough of Haringey	14 January 1972
Crawley Urban District Council	14 January 1972
Coventry County Borough Council	3 February 1972
Birmingham County Borough Council	4 February 1972
Meriden Rural District Council	4 February 1972
Newcastle-upon-Tyne County Borough Council	10 February 1972
Northumberland County Council	11 February 1972
Seaton Valley Urban District Council	11 February 1972
Liverpool County Borough Council	17 February 1972
Winsford Urban District Council	18 February 1972
Stockport County Borough Council	16 February 1972
Cardiff County Borough Council	24 February 1972
Rhondda Borough Council	25 February 1972
Neath Rural District Council	25 February 1972
Montgomery County Council	25 February 1972
Bradford County Borough Council	2 March 1972
Leeds County Borough Council	3 March 1972
Monmouth Borough Council	19 April 1972

Appendix E

Oral evidence
list of witnesses

Mr F J C Amos, BSc(Soc), DipArch, SPDip, ARIBA, MTPI, City Planner of Liverpool County Borough Council

Mr S R Barnes, Director of the Local Authorities Management Services and Computer Committee

Bradford Telegraph and Argus, Representatives of

Mr P J Coomber, FIMTA, DPA, Chief Executive and Town Clerk of the London Borough of Ealing

Mr A G Dawtry, CBE, TD, LLB, Town Clerk and Chief Executive, Westminster City Council; Secretary, London Boroughs' Association

Mr R L Doble, MA, Chief Executive and Town Clerk of the London Borough of Greenwich

Mr L Evans, MIPR, Head of the Local Government Information Office

Mr J D Hender, FIMTA, FCA, Chief Executive and Town Clerk of Coventry County Borough Council

Miss J Long, BCom, PhD, jointly with Mr A Norton, MA (Cantab), MSocSc, Institute of Local Government Studies University of Birmingham.

Management Consultants Association

Mr R H McCall, OBE, Town Clerk and Chief Executive Officer of Winchester City Council

Mr D S Mumford, Personnel Manager, Imperial Chemical Industries Ltd

National and Local Government Officers Association

Mr R Nottage, CMG, Director of the Royal Institute of Public Administration

Royal Institute of British Architects

Mr W W Ruff, DL, Clerk of Surrey County Council

Sheffield Polytechnic—Centre for Management Studies

Society of Education Officers

Professor J D Stewart, DPhil, MA, Associate Director at the Institute of Local Government Studies University of Birmingham

Mr D H Taylor, Town Manager and Clerk of Basildon Urban District Council

Mr J B Woodham, BSc(Econ), FIMTA, Treasurer of Teesside County Borough Council

Appendix F

The following officers were invited to serve as advisers to the Working Group:—

Clerks and Town Clerks

Mr J M Carter LLM, (Whiston RDC)
Mr S Holmes DL, (Liverpool CBC)
Mr R E Millard LLB, (Buckinghamshire CC)
Mr W W Ruff DL, (Surrey CC)
Mr T Scholes MC, LLB, (Maidstone BC)
Mr M Shawcross (Woking UDC)

Treasurers

Mr T A Bird BSc, (Econ), FIMTA, (Cambridge BC)
Mr J S Blackburn BA (Admin), FIMTA (Leicestershire CC)
Mr R H A Chisholm CBE, FIMTA, (Cheshire CC)
Mr J Huxley FIMTA, FCA, (Wellingborough UDC)
Mr R H Moores BSc (Econ), FIMTA, (New Forest RDC)
Mr F Tolson (Leeds CBC)

Education

Mr S T Broad MA, CBE (Hertfordshire CC)
Mr L J Drew MA, MEd, (Swansea CBC)
Mr D A Fiske MA, (Manchester CBC)
Mr J Haynes MA, DCL, (Kent CC)

Engineers and Surveyors

Mr A T Bennett* CEng, MICE, FIMunE, MInstHE, MBIM (Sevenoaks UDC)
Mr N Borg CEng, FICE, FIMunE (Birmingham CBC)
Mr P C Gane FICE, MIHE (Lindsey CC)
Mr S W Harvey CEng, FIMunE, FIPHE, MIWE, AMIHE, MBIM,
(Chelmsford RDC)
Mr W T Luke* BSc, CEng., MICE., MIHE, (Gelligaer UDC)
Mr S N Mustow BSc, CEng (Stoke-on-Trent CBC)
Mr J W Radcliffe MEng, CEng, FICE, FIMunE, MTPI, MBIM, AIAS
(Teesside CBC)
Mr W R Thomson FICE, FIMunE, FInstHE (Worcestershire CC)
Mr D S Warren CEng, FICE, FIMunE, FGS (Dudley CBC)

Lighting Engineer

Mr H Carpenter CEng, FIEE, FIllumES, FAPLE, (Blackpool CBC)

Planning

Mr J H Barratt MSc, DipTP, MTPI, (Staffordshire CC)
Mr F W Dawkes BSc (Eng), MICE, FIMunE, FRTPI, (Bedford BC)
Mr E Parkinson BSc, DPA, MTPI, MICE, MIMunE, (Cardiff CBC)
Mr E G Sibert MTPI, FRICS, (Surrey CC)

Architects

Mr B C Adams FRIBA, (Somerset CC)
Mr G C Fardell MBE, FRIBA, (Hertfordshire CC)
Mr R H Fleming DipArch, ARIBA, DipTP, (Huyton-with-Roby UDC)
Mr T W Gregory OBE, FRIBA, FRICS, FRTPI, (Coventry CBC)
Mr W R Hazelwood ARIBA, AMTPI, (South Cambridgeshire RDC)
Mr E E Hollamby OBE, FRIBA, MTPI, DipTP (Lond), (Lambeth LBC)

Social Services

Mr W E Boyce OBE, FISW, (Essex CC)
Mr J H Gardham DMA, FISW, (Kingston upon Hull CBC)

Mr S R J Terry (Kingston upon Thames LBC)

Miss S B Watson OBE, MA, (Cambridgeshire and Isle of Ely CC)

Medical Officers

Mr A J Essex-Cater MD, MRCS, LRCP, DPH, DTH, FRAI, FSCF, (Monmouthshire CC)

Mr A Gatherer MD, ChB, DPH, DIH, (Reading CBC)

Mr R E A S Hansen MA, MB, BChir, DPH, (Stroud RDC)

Mr W G Harding FRCP, FFCM, DPH, (Camden LBC)

Mr J B Kershaw MB, BS, MRCS, LRSP, DPH, (Hinckley UDC)

Mr G Ramage MA (Admin), MD, BSc, MB, ChB, DPH, MRCS, LRCP, (Staffordshire CC)

Police

Sir Derrick Capper QPM, (Chief Constable of Birmingham City Police Force)

Sir Douglas Osmond CBE, QPM, BSc, (Chief Constable of Hampshire Police Authority)

Sir John Willison OBE, QPM, DL, (Chief Constable of West Mercia Police Authority)

Fire

Mr D Blacktop OBE, AMIFireE (Staffordshire CC)

Mr J H Helm MBE, (Solihull CBC)

Mr F Taylor CBE, QFSM Grad IFireE (Liverpool CBC)

Mr J B Vickery OBE (Surrey CC)

Housing

Mr H J Aldhous OBE, BSc, ARICS, FIHM, (Sheffield CBC)

Mr F H Blake AIHM, ARSH, (Milford Haven UDC)

Mr A C Gittins FIHM, FRSH, ARICS, (St Faith's and Aylsham RDC)

Mr P E Hargreaves AIHM, (Leamington Spa BC)

Quantity Surveyor

Mr H C Morris FRICS (Nottinghamshire CC)

Building Manager

Mr W L Pearson FIMunBM (Barking LBC)

Public Health

Mr B D Allen DPA, FAPHI, MRSH, (Coventry CBC)
Mr F G Caudery** FAPHI, MRSH, (Amersham RDC)
Mr J Skitt FInstPC, FIPlantE, MIRTE (Stoke-on-Trent CBC)
Mr A J Stroud FRSH, FAPHI, (Wellingborough UDC)
Mr E N Wakelin OBE, FAPHI, FRSH, (Birmingham CBC)

Consumer Protection

Mr F M Bucknall DPA, FIWMA, FISAA, DSAA, (Grimsby CBC)
Mr F J Evans DPA, MIWMA, (Northamptonshire CC)
Mr D W Johnson DPA, FIWMA, MInstPET, (Slough BC)
Mr W K Natrass DPA, MIWMA, (Cheshire CC)
Mr P S Roberts MIWMA, (Huyton-with-Roby UDC)

Land Agents/Valuers

Mr C D Dutton ARICS, FRGS, (Brighton CBC)
Mr J P Fellows*** FSVA, FRVA, (Wrexham RDC)
Mr C J H Kaye ARICS, (Havant and Waterloo UDC)
Mr F Longdon BSc, FRICS, (Manchester CBC)
Mr D G Merriot FRICS, (Hertfordshire CC)
Mr C H Moore FRICS, (Gloucestershire CC)

Libraries

Mr R F Ashby FLA, (Surrey CC)
Mr C Dyson ALA, (Runcorn UDC)
Mr F Hallworth FLA, FRGS, (Wiltshire CC)
Mr P D Pocklington FLA, (Chester CBC)
Mr G P Rye FLA, (Weston-super-Mare BC)

Museums

Mr F T Baker OBE, MA, FSA, (Lincoln CBC)
Mr K J Barton FSA, FMA, (Portsmouth CBC)

Parks and Amenities

Mr H Charlesworth MBE, ERD, FIPHE, FRSH, (Easthampstead RDC)
Mr L W Davies MInstRM, (Basildon UDC)
Mr R V C Joyner LInstPA, MInstBCA, FRHS, (Warley CBC)
Mr R Vann ALA, (Redditch UDC)
Mr A L Winning FInstPRA(Dip), NDH, MInstBCA, MInst RM
(Sheffield CBC)

Supplies

Mr D J Ewart FInstPS, (Liverpool CBC)
Mr C F Rix MInstPS, (Wiltshire CC)

Transportation

Mr A G Burrows FCIT, (Director General Merseyside Passenger
Transport Executive)
Mr H G Ludlow AMInstT, (Pontypridd UDC)
Mr L H Smith TD, DL, MInstT, (Leicester CBC)

  * Also an adviser on planning.
 ** Also an adviser on consumer protection.
*** Also an adviser on housing.

Appendix G

The Bradford Plan

In 1968 Bradford C.B.C. introduced far reaching changes in their management structure and it was intended that the changes should encompass the following objectives:—

"(i) a recognisable logical pattern of delegation, with details readily accessible;

(ii) a considerable decrease in the number of decisions formally made at Council and in committee;

(iii) an increase in the deliberative and significant policy making function at Council and in committee with a diminution in political attitudes and disputation over matters of minimal importance;

(iv) more positive co-ordination of functions;

(v) a substantial reduction in the time spent by officers and members in preparation for and attendance at, committee".

So far as the laying down of a logical pattern of delegation of their powers and duties, this led to the following general pattern—

Council—to deal only with the matters which by statute cannot be delegated (e.g. levying of a rate) and such matters as are referred to it by a committee.

Committees (5)—to deal with major policy matters and matters of importance because of their controversial nature.

Special Sub-Committees (5)—to deal with matters of a programmed routine nature where a decision must, by law, be formally made and to deal with any matter as a case of urgency.

Chief Officers—to deal with all operational management matters of a service activity and any matter in an emergency.

In addition, the Council introduced a system of Executive Groups. In the report leading up to the introduction of the new management structure it was stated—

"It is also important ... to ensure a wide spread of responsibility amongst members. It is, therefore, recommended ... that the Council should grant authority to small groups of members to deal with particular service activities ... in this way it will be possible for every member of the Council to be involved in the decision-making process at all levels where democratic control is desirable and for decisions to be reached with the minimum of delay. This should make the role of the ordinary member of Council much more meaningful and worthwhile".

It was also stated in the report that—

"The convener, deputy convener and members of an executive group together with the appropriate Chief Officer will deal with other than the operational management of a service activity. Operational management is the responsibility of the Chief Officer and his staff but the decision link in day to day matters not requiring formal record will be dealt with within the executive group. Their proceedings will not require the attendance of committee clerks and the minimal amount of record will be made by the Chief Officer to reduce paper work. In the event of disagreement as to course of action, the matter occasioning the disagreement must be made an agenda item for decision at committee level".

It should be noted that the Chief Officer is a full participant in the deliberations of an executive group and is in exactly the same position as a member. Thus, in the event of a disagreement between the Chief Officer and the other members of an executive group, the Chief Officer can refer the subject matter of the disagreement to the parent committee for decision.

Each committee divides its membership into executive groups, a member serving on not more than two groups. The Chairman and the Deputy Chairman of Committees are not normally members of executive groups but may attend a meeting of an executive group at any time if they so wish.

The responsibilities of the groups vary according to their individual subject matter but all have the following powers and duties:—

a   Generally

> **1**   to determine appeals or complaints relating to decisions made by the appropriate Chief Officer in accordance with powers or duties delegated to him;

> **2**   to consider and make recommendations to the appropriate Committee upon any matters in relation to which the Council have powers or duties or which affect the City;

> **3**   to determine any matters referred by the appropriate Chief Officer which have not been determined under powers or duties delegated to him.

b   On the advice of the appropriate Chief Officer

> **1**   to approve exceptions to schemes of general policy approved by the Council or the appropriate committee;
> **2**   to accept other than the lowest tender for goods, services or other matters where payment is to be made by the Council, or other than the highest tender where payment is to be received by the Council;

> **3**   to authorise variations in the contractual rights or obligations of the Council and to refer disputes to arbitration;

> **4**   to approve plans for the modification or construction of buildings;

> **5**   to vary the hours or days during which buildings or services shall be available to the public;

> **6**   to determine charges and fees for services and licences;

7 to accept quotations exceeding £5,000;

8 to determine the names of Corporation premises;

9 to approve negotiations for the purchase, sale or leasing of land where such sale, purchase or lease has been approved in principle by the appropriate committee, provided that (a) the negotiated price is not in excess of £10,000 or the annual rent is not in excess of £1,000 and (b) where terms have been negotiated under a specific decision of the appropriate committee, that that decision is not more than twelve months before the negotiated terms are reported for approval;

10 to approve negotiations for the leasing of land required for gas governor sites to the North Eastern Gas Board and for sub-station sites to the Yorkshire Electricity Board.

In addition to these delegated powers and duties, the executive groups are a forum where there can be informal discussion on any matter and where future policy can be informally discussed for the first time between the members and the Chief Officers.

In 1968 the subject matter for each group was chosen largely on the previous pattern of service committees. Since then a pattern more closely related to the major interests of the parent committees is emerging and groups like 'Transportation' or 'Community Services' are proving worthwhile. If local government reorganisation had not been imminent, it is likely that this process of assigning segments of a programme area to executive groups would have been expedited.

In order to assist in preventing the executive groups from becoming 'sub-committees', they have met informally in a Chief Officer's room or 'on location' and they do not have a formal agenda or formal minutes. Again the use of the term 'Chairman' has been avoided and the term 'Convener' substituted.

The Press inspect the 'decisions' of the executive groups once each week and the 'decisions' are available for inspection by all members of the Council. At meetings of the parent committee, the convener of an executive group has an opportunity to bring to the committee's attention any particular 'decision' of the executive group.

Appendix H

Terms of reference for a policy and resources committee

a To guide the Council in the formulation of its corporate plan of objectives and priorities, and for this purpose to recommend to the council such forward programmes and other steps as may be necessary to achieve those objectives, either in whole or in part, during specific time spans. For this purpose to consider the broad social and economic needs of the authority and matters of comprehensive importance to the area including the contents of structure plans. To advise the Council generally as to its financial and economic policies.

b Without prejudice to the duties and responsibilities of the programme committees, to review the effectiveness of all the Council's work and the standards and levels of service provided. To identify the need for new services and to keep under review the necessity for existing ones.

c To submit to the Council concurrent reports with the programme committees upon new policies or changes in policy formulated by such committees, particularly those which may have significant impact upon the corporate plan or the resources of the Council.

d To be responsible for allocating and controlling the financial, manpower and land resources of the Council.

e To ensure that the organisation and management processes of the council are designed to make the most effective contribution to the achievement of the Council's objectives. To keep them under review in the light of changing circumstances, making recommendations as necessary for change in either the committee or departmental structure, or the distribution of functions and responsibilities.

f To be concerned together with the appropriate programme committee in the appointment of Heads of Departments and any Deputies.

Appendix J

Job specification for a Chief Executive

1   The Chief Executive is the head of the Council's paid service and shall have authority over all other officers so far as this is necessary for the efficient management and execution of the Council's functions.

2   He is the leader of the officers' management team and through the Policy and Resources Committee, the Council's principal adviser on matters of general policy. As such it is his responsibility to secure co-ordination of advice on the forward planning of objectives and services and to lead the management team in securing a corporate approach to the affairs of the authority generally.

3   Through his leadership of the officers' management team he is responsible for the efficient and effective implementation of the Council's programmes and policies and for securing that the resources of the authority are most effectively deployed towards those ends.

4   Similarly he shall keep under review the organisation and administration of the authority and shall make recommendations to the Council through the Policy and Resources Committee if he considers that major changes are required in the interests of effective management.

5   As head of the paid service it is his responsibility to ensure that effective and equitable manpower policies are developed and implemented throughout all departments of the authority in the interests both of the authority and the staff.

6   He is responsible for the maintenance of good internal and external relations.

Appendix K

Activities undertaken by Local Authority Public Relations, Press and Information Departments or Sections

Press Relations

Liaison with sound broadcasting and television

Press monitoring service for Principal Officers

Civic Bulletins

Information Centre, Bureau or Service

Telephone Information Service

Complaints Service (about Council services)

Liaison with local organisations

Provision of lectures, speakers etc. for local organisations

Organisation of visits of groups to Council meetings

Facility visits to Council establishments

Welcome to Citizenship for new 18-year-old voters

Special activities such as Council *Brains Trust, Any Questions* sessions, Town Forums, Open Days, Public Participation meetings, etc.

Publications and leaflets

Preparation of Council Annual Reports

Preparation, printing and posting of posters, notices etc., on authority's poster and notice boards

Local Government or departmental exhibitions or displays

Production of films

Production or circulation of visual aids about civic activities (e.g. transparencies, slides, filmstrips etc.)

Promotion of teaching of civics in schools

Staff recruitment advertising

Staff handbooks or staff magazine

Staff training in public relations

Public Opinion or Attitude Research

Resort or Town Publicity

Industrial Development

Civic Entertainments

Organisation of civic events (e.g. Mayor Making, Mayor's Charity Ball etc.)

Town's Engagement Diary—*What's On*

Specialised Publicity (e.g. Municipal Airport, Docks etc.)

Appendix L

Allocation of main functions

Non-Metropolitan Counties

Social Services and Personal Health Services
        Social Services

Education and Related Services
        Education
        Libraries
        Museums and Art Galleries (c)

Housing and Town Development
        Certain reserve powers, eg overspill
        Town Development

Town and Country Planning and Related Matters
        Structure Plans
        Local Plans (in special cases)
        Development Control (strategic and reserved decisions)
        Acquisition and disposal of land for planning purposes, developments or redevelopment (c)
        Clearance of derelict land (c)
        National Parks (subject to existence of boards)
        Country Parks (c)
        Footpaths and Bridleways
        Commons—registration
        Caravan Sites—provision (c)
        Gipsy Sites—provision
        Smallholdings and Cottage Holdings

Non-Metropolitan Districts

Education and Related Services
      Museums and Art Galleries (c)

Housing and Town Development
      Housing
      Town Development

Town and Country Planning and Related Matters
      Local Plans (most)
      Development Control (most)
      Acquisition and disposal of land for planning purposes, development or redevelopment (c)
      Clearance of derelict land (c)
      Country Parks (c)
      Footpaths and Bridleways
      Caravan Sites—provision (c)
      licensing and management
      Gipsy Sites—management
      Allotments

Highways and Related Subjects

> Transport Planning
>
> Highways—all (subject to the rights of districts to claim powers)
> Traffic
>
> Parking
>
> Public Transport Undertakings (co-ordination)
>
> Road Safety
>
> Street Lighting

Consumer Protection

> Weights and Measures
>
> Food and Drugs
>
> Trade Descriptions
>
> Consumer Protection Act 1961
>
> etc

Other Environmental Services

> Land Drainage
>
> Refuse Disposal
>
> Health Education (c)

Highways and Related Subjects

Highways—right to claim maintenance powers in relation to unclassified roads in urban areas

Public Transport Undertakings—operation

Environmental Health

Food Safety and Hygiene

Control of Communicable Disease

Offices, Shops and Railway Premises Act

Factories Act

Shops Act

etc

Other Environmental Services

Local Sewers

Land Drainage

Refuse Collection
Litter

Coast Protection
Clean Air

Building Regulations

Street Cleansing

Police and Fire

Police (subject to amalgamation)

Fire

Recreation and Tourism

Swimming Baths (c)

Parks and open spaces (c)

Physical training and recreation (c)

Licensing and Registration Functions

Births, Deaths and Marriages

Adoption Societies

etc

Other Services

Entertainments (c)

Aerodromes (c)

Natural Emergencies (c)

Nuisances

Cemeteries and Crematoria

Markets

Offensive Trades

Health Education (c)

etc

Recreation and Tourism

Swimming Baths (c)

Parks and open spaces (c)

Physical training and recreation (c)

Publicity for tourist attractions

Licensing and Registration Functions

Most

Other Services

Entertainments (c)

Aerodromes (c)

Natural Emergencies (c)

c = concurrent functions

Metropolitan Counties

Education and Related Services
> Museums and Art Galleries (c)

Housing and Town Development
> Certain reserve powers, eg overspill
> Town Development

Town and Country Planning and Related Matters
> Structure Plans
> Local Plans (in special cases)
> Development Control (strategic and reserved decisions)
> Acquisition and disposal of land for planning purposes, development or redevelopment (c)
> Clearance of derelict land (c)
> National Parks (subject to existence of boards)
> Country Parks (c)
> Footpaths and Bridleways
> Commons—registration
> Caravan Sites—provision (c)
> Gipsy Sites—provision
> Smallholdings and Cottage Holdings

Highways and Related Subjects
> Transport Planning
> Highways—all (subject to the rights of districts to claim powers)
> Traffic

Metropolitan Districts

Social Services and Personal Health Services
        Social Services

Education and Related Services
        Education
        Libraries
        Museums and Art Galleries (c)

Housing and Town Development
        Housing
        Town Development

Town and Country Planning and Related Matters
        Local Plans (most)
        Development Control (most)
        Acquisition and disposal of land for planning purposes, development or redevelopment (c)
        Clearance of derelict land (c)
        Country Parks (c)
        Footpaths and Bridleways
        Commons—management
        Caravan Sites—provision (c) licensing and management
        Gipsy Sites—management

Highways and Related Subjects
        Highways—right to claim maintenance powers in relation to unclassified roads in urban areas

Parking
Passenger Transport Authorities
Road Safety

Consumer Protection

Weights and Measures
Food and Drugs
Trade Descriptions
Consumer Protection Act 1961
etc

Other Environmental Services

Land Drainage
Refuse Disposal
Health Education

Police and Fire

Police (subject to amalgamation)
Fire (subject to amalgamation)

Environmental Health

> Food Safety and Hygiene
> Control of Communicable Disease
> Offices, Shops and Railway Premises Act
> Factories Act
> Shops Act
> etc

Other Environmental Services

> Local sewers
> Land Drainage
> Refuse Collection
> Litter
> Coast Protection
> Clean Air
> Building Regulations
> Nuisances
> Cemeteries and Crematoria
> Markets
> Offensive Trades
> Health Education (c)

Recreation and Tourism
>
> Swimming Baths (c)
>
> Parks and open spaces (c)
>
> Physical training and recreation (c)

Other Services

> Entertainments (c)
>
> Aerodromes (c)
>
> Natural Emergencies (c)

Recreation and Tourism

        Swimming Baths (c)

        Parks and open spaces (c)

        Physical training and recreation (c)

        Publicity for tourist attractions

Licensing and Registration Functions

        Most

Other Services

        Entertainments (c)

        Aerodromes (c)

        Natural Emergencies (c)

---

c = concurrent functions

Printed in England for Her Majesty's Stationery Office
by Kent County Council, Supplies Department, Maidstone

Dd 505578 K 400 7/72

HER MAJESTY'S STATIONERY OFFICE

Government Bookshops

49 High Holborn, London WC1V 6HB
13a Castle Street, Edinburgh EH2 3AR
109 St Mary Street, Cardiff CF1 1JW
Brazennose Street, Manchester M60 8AS
50 Fairfax Street, Bristol BS1 3DE
528 Broad Street, Birmingham B1 2HE
80 Chichester Street, Belfast BT1 4JY

*Government publications are also available
through booksellers*

£1 Net